GW01163825

Discovering Your Mastery

UNLOCKING HIDDEN CODES WITHIN

Leni Morrison and Jilliana Raymond

BALBOA.PRESS
A DIVISION OF HAY HOUSE

Copyright © 2021 Leni Morrison and Jilliana Raymond.

All rights reserved. No part of this book may be used or reproduced by any means, graphic, electronic, or mechanical, including photocopying, recording, taping or by any information storage retrieval system without the written permission of the author except in the case of brief quotations embodied in critical articles and reviews.

Balboa Press books may be ordered through booksellers or by contacting:

Balboa Press
A Division of Hay House
1663 Liberty Drive
Bloomington, IN 47403
www.balboapress.com
844-682-1282

Because of the dynamic nature of the Internet, any web addresses or links contained in this book may have changed since publication and may no longer be valid. The views expressed in this work are solely those of the author and do not necessarily reflect the views of the publisher, and the publisher hereby disclaims any responsibility for them.

The author of this book does not dispense medical advice or prescribe the use of any technique as a form of treatment for physical, emotional, or medical problems without the advice of a physician, either directly or indirectly. The intent of the author is only to offer information of a general nature to help you in your quest for emotional and spiritual well-being. In the event you use any of the information in this book for yourself, which is your constitutional right, the author and the publisher assume no responsibility for your actions.

Any people depicted in stock imagery provided by Getty Images are models, and such images are being used for illustrative purposes only.
Certain stock imagery © Getty Images.

Interior Graphics/Art Credit: Shutterstock, Teo Tarras, Quantum

All Scriptures taken from the King James version of The Bible

Print information available on the last page.

ISBN: 978-1-9822-7312-5 (sc)
ISBN: 978-1-9822-7313-2 (hc)
ISBN: 978-1-9822-7314-9 (e)

Library of Congress Control Number: 2021916833

Balboa Press rev. date: 09/10/2021

The words within these pages are light infused.
Their role is to heal, empower and provide ascension codes
for all those ready to embody the vibration of light.
Take only the words that resonate within your heart,
allowing all others to unfold within the realm of
Divine timing or simply fall away.

Preface
How It Began

Leni Morrison – A Personal Story

I was in Australia teaching academic English to Third Level Asian students at RMIT University in Melbourne. I was 24, had pillar box red hair and not a care in the world. I was absolutely thriving in this city! I was renting a penthouse, earning top dollars and, I was so incredibly happy that I was seriously considering moving my life 'Down Under'.

One evening, out of the blue, my brother Michael called me. He pretty much convinced me that I needed to get on the next plane out of Oz and head over to Brazil. He was staying at a healing retreat in Brazil experiencing some amazing results with his own healing journey. It was here that he met a powerful medium from New York. Her name was Julie and she insisted that I get down to the center and leave Australia immediately. She spoke to me on the phone and left me with little doubt I had a life changing adventure ahead of me in South America. So next thing I know I am navigating my way through the dusty windy mountainous terrain of Goias Brazil. Goodbye penthouse and 'hello donkey' tied to the side of a tree.

The healing center was located in the Crystal Mountains of Abadiania. As soon as I touched base with my brother, I was shown to my Pousada (hostel) where I finally met Julie. She was a "Daughter of the Casa." Her role was to mentor new arrivals. After eating a feast of feijoada (Brazilian black bean stew), I was advised to go to bed early as I would need sleep for the big day ahead of me. Julie told me to meet her at 5:30 am. She informed me to be dressed all in white and be outside my pousada at that time. She would then take me to the healing center and advise me on all the rituals.

I tried to sleep that first night, but I kept hearing the voice of a man speaking loudly in what I assumed was Spanish throughout the night. The voice was so real. I was certain he was in the room with me. Every time I turned on a light there was no one there. I put my overactive imagination down to jetlag.

Julie arrived in the morning to escort me to the healing center as planned. There were hundreds of people from around the world queuing to meet the healer. As I got closer to the healer, he popped his head out to look through the line of people in front of him to look directly at me--and pointed. Julie turned around and in her thick Bronx accent said "Oh boy, he recognizes you. This is going to be fun!" I panicked. To say my heart was racing was a huge understatement.

The remarks from the healer to all those ahead of me were of a loving, gentle nature. But as soon as I passed before him he started shouting at me in anger in a language I knew to be Spanish. Was this the same voice I had heard the night before? Suddenly I was placed beside him and instructed to sit on a bean bag on the stage. I was told to stay there with my eyes closed until the morning session had finished. This was another four hours.

While on the stage in my personal silence with my eyes closed I had a complete life review. I witnessed times in this life that I nearly died through my own misadventures. I also reviewed what I now believe were my past lives. I was aware at times of being on what I presumed were other dimensions and on other worlds. While all of this was going on internally, I was intrigued that I could smell what could only be described as anesthetic. I could also feel what I thought was a constant trickle of perspiration running down my chest. It was summer in Brazil. What else could it be?

The morning session had finally ended. I still had my eyes closed as instructed. The room emptied, except for me, Julie, the healer and two of his team. Julie informed me that during the time I had been seated next to the healer I received what was called "psychic surgery". It was explained that my heart had been broken so many lifetimes that it was necessary to remove depression and ancestral pain from previous life insults. Julie told me not to freak out when I opened my eyes, as my previously white dress was now streaked in blood. The psychic surgery was painless. Interestingly, the surgery was performed by a Spanish doctor. Could the voice that kept me awake all night have been that same doctor? My mind was completely blown, and I'm Irish! The Irish are steeped in faery folklore, Celtic shamanism, and the odd banshee—but this—this was brand new territory.

The healer told me I too was to become a "Daughter of the Casa," and my new role at the age of 24 was to inform people from around the world about sacred divine and cosmic healing power. He also told me that one day I would be doing this type of energy work. I would go back and forth over the next few years and learn much from this miracle worker and the countless incredible shamans and teachers in that community.

During this meeting I was gifted with two large powerful crystals from the Abadiania Mountains, which I work with to this day. This profound experience began a deeply exciting lifelong journey into the unknown worlds of quantum healing, as well as a deeper connection and understanding of the crystalline pathways of mother earth.

Jilliana Raymond

I find it interesting that some of the greatest channelers and spiritual leaders began their spiritual exploration as extreme skeptics. Prior to embarking on their own spiritual adventures, these incredible leaders held positions as engineers, scientists, contractors, and medical researchers, with many coming from two schools of traditional thought: religious or agnostic beliefs. Most had no exposure to spiritual anything. In fact, most attendees participated in a spiritual event at the encouragement from a trusted individual's insistence. Many were thrown into the realm of energy having no idea what that meant. Few, if any, had any previous awareness of some latent intuitive ability or ability to connect to any spiritual force. Again, their thoughts could at times seem like "nonsense," even downright scary for the new initiate.

My first encounter with anything other worldly began following the death of my mother. I remember waking one night to visualize her floating form enter my room, expressing to me that everything would be alright. There was no audible sound heard but a deep "knowing" this was the message she was delivering. She wore a mint green chiffon gown, appearing to me as she might have appeared around the age of 30. (I have since learned the age of 30 seems to be a popular presentation for those who have passed and return to the physical realm to visit loved ones.) I am a rather logical person, so this presentation, although very real, seemed extraordinarily unexplainable. I might add I came from a staunchly religious background. I am also the type of person that needs rational answers. Certainly, this experience was anything but rational. Thus began my research into the unfamiliar "spiritual" side of things.

I enrolled in any class I could find that would provide any kind of answer to satisfy my natural curiosity. My religious training had not prepared me for anything so unbelievable or so enticing. My first experience with energy occurred after enrolling in a Reiki class. Reiki was a popular area of study at the time, and I had a previous experience with the teacher, so I decided to explore this modality. I followed the instructions carefully, musing over the excited outbursts from participants marveling as they felt the energy. I felt nothing! Not one to give in, I enrolled in the same class again. I had a medical background so I was interested in anything that had to do with healing. I was determined to experience the sensation many others were exclaiming delight in. Again, I felt nothing. And again, determined to discover what so many were experiencing, and at the urging of the instructor, I enrolled in this Reiki class a third time. There is a saying "third times the charm." And so it was. I felt the energy, what everyone else was so excited about. The energy was faint at first, nevertheless definitely detectable. This encounter was nearly thirty years ago. I would spend the next four years studying with the class instructor who as it turned out was a healing master. Today I am considered an intuitive energy channel, spiritual adviser, and alternative therapy master. I tell this story to my audiences to demonstrate that your inherent talents exist within you, even if you are unaware of your hidden abilities.

I have been privileged to experience other dimensional realities that to most would be unbelievable, yet mesmerizing and awesome beyond belief. There is nothing extraordinary about me other than my innate curiosity and tenacity not to give up. You possess the same ability to experience the spiritual dimension as I do. It is my wish that all could begin to experience some form of phenomenal energy that would awaken their curiosity to explore the dimensions I have been privy to. My encounters are personal and yet very real. My discoveries are proof of life beyond any physical existence. It is my belief all will experience some encounter with energy awakening and begin their personal exploration into their own personal accumulative life experiences. I can only promise that if you are open to new presenting concepts you will be wildly intrigued to begin your own cosmic exploration into who you really are. Once you begin your exploration you will learn how you can utilize energy to your advantage and become aware of a cosmic connection to spiritual resources that will assist in optimizing your physical journey during this life.

Contents

Preface – How It Began..vii

Introduction xv

Thoughts to Ponder... 1

The Quantum Tapestry... 5

Ancestral Healing... 17

Non-Conflict Resolution.. 31

Non-Conflict Meditation... 37

Power of Your Word... 41

Learning to Love Yourself.. 55

What Makes You Who You Are? 65

What Makes You Who You Are 77

Life from a Higher Perspective 81

How to Receive Messages of Light.. 89

Vibrational Resonance 101

Who's in Your Soul Family?... 115

Connecting with Your Inner Child.. 125

Your Conscious Universe 133

Solar Logos 143
Dimensions 149
The Emerald Codes 153
For Your Contemplation 165

About the Authors 175
Research Credits 177
Glossary 181
Author Resources 189
Author Resources 193

Introduction

Misconception, ritual, and tradition often contribute to individual belief systems including how to communicate with a spiritual source. With many differing thoughts, one might even wonder if a divine resource exists. To present a new perception into the universal forces that align with earth consciousness and the life upon this incredible planet, an eight-month information series was born and presented to an international group of wisdom seekers. The series was so successful, the decision to present the information to a public audience via written modality was made. You are about to receive a compilation of the presented information with additional wisdom teachings within these pages.

The international audience acknowledged a profoundly transformational understanding of their individual roles while exploring their deeply personal physical journeys within a spiritual universe. Participants acknowledged the wisdom received would greatly change the way each would view and now change their lives in extraordinary ways. Lifelong emotional traumas were released, a renewed connectivity to universal forces was established, exhilaration for life was revitalized and an understanding of how extraordinary everyone's life truly is was becoming apparent. This is the information you are about to assimilate by reading the sequence of information presented within these pages.

Here is a well thought compilation of spiritual wisdom launched by two spiritual teachers/healers, Leni Morrison and Jilliana Raymond. Their commitment is to reveal the spiritual heritage of every living soul. The insight will provide information on how to activate every individual's sovereign connection to a spiritual universe.

Thoughts to Ponder

Jilliana Raymond

WHAT IF EVERYTHING YOU THOUGHT YOU KNOW ABOUT YOUR LIVING world didn't work quite like you were taught to believe? How would you go about researching a new paradigm that was in better alignment with a new world? I'm a realist or at least I like to think so. While my curiosity remains open to new concepts, I haven't always embraced change gracefully. I have also resisted new thought ideations that broke from my traditional childhood teachings but my stubborn perseverance led me to research every element presented within the writings I present to my audiences.

Many rely on historic texts to resolve their curiosity. We should learn from historic anthologies but interpretations can be molded to present directives designed to provide steerage for that era. How else can we explore our living world? At first I read any material I thought would provide intriguing insight. I'd ponder the information, test it, if you will, experiment and research every avenue I thought might provide some element of truth to the presented concept. This book is in part a compilation of years of research, curiosity and resolution to the profound wisdom that awaits the adventurer.

There is no test, just a lot of thoughts to ponder. You may find some potential answers within these pages. Your own personal research may lead you to discover more. What is certain is your lineage is ancient. The complexity of your soul is extensive. The extent of the universe in which you reside is infinite and life eternal.

Who or what is God?

Does God hear my prayers?

Are there really angels?

What do angels look like?

Why do I encounter challenges in my life?

If God is so divine why is there so much suffering, violence and war?

How can I choose a better way of living?

If I am creating my living experience every day, why do I create trauma?

I've heard that everything I do in my life matters and how I conduct my life determines how I will experience my life in spirit. What might I change in my life, if anything?

If my life experience is a scripted drama, why did I choose my current life role?

If I have a life purpose, what is it?

Why did I choose to master my current role?

I have read that earth is a planet of free choice. If this is true, did I choose my parents?

If I chose my parents, why?

If my vibration allows me access to higher dimensions, how can I increase my vibration?

If life is eternal, do I have any past lives?

If I have any past lives, what were they?

Are there other planets with life on them?

If there are multiverses, how many are there, and what might be the differences between them?

If there is life on other planets, what do the inhabitants look like?

Could I come from a distant planet?

If my home planet isn't earth, what planet did I come from?

Is there life after death?

What happens when I die?

What does life in spirit look like?

These questions were what launched my initial research and helped satisfy some of my curiosity. But I suspect if you find an answer to any one of these questions it will astound you and ignite your desire to discover more of the secrets of the universe. Mastering just one principle can change your life. It certainly did mine.

The Quantum Tapestry

Jilliana Raymond

THE UNIVERSE IS A MAGICAL ENVIRONMENT. HOW WE INTERACT WITH spiritual resources can often feel secretive, illusive, and even forbidden. But this couldn't be further from the truth. My goal is to shed light on some misgivings and unlock some of the mysteries of the universe in which you reside.

We should first explore what happens when you initiate spiritual solicitation. Have you ever wondered what happens when you pray or when a group prayer is delivered? Have you pondered who hears your prayerful solicitations, how your prayers are received, or even whether they are answered? Would you like to meet those individuals who surround you on a continuous basis? The answers to these questions are forthcoming.

You may have a working knowledge of the mechanics solicited on your behalf with any invocation, but I would like to give you a broader window into the technical components that go into motion the moment you enter any solicitation. You are going to discover how magnificent the universe can be.

Every time you generate a prayer or spiritual solicitation there is a network of activity arranged on your behalf. No prayer or request is too insignificant to solicit a response. I have clients who tell me their request is too insignificant to "bother" a divine force with. *Nothing is too insignificant.* Every prayer is important, no matter how simple or trivial it may seem. If you want to create a parking space or arrange for a special ticket for an event you want to attend, it's okay to ask. There is no limit to the number of requests you can solicit. If it is important to you—it is important to the universe. Rule number one then, is to eliminate any ideation that there are a limited number of requests you can make or that you should save those prayers for something enormously important. Nonsense.

Depending upon the country you reside within, it is most likely you have grown up with cultural and/or religious parameters. This foundation certainly provides guidance on the way you communicate within your cultural community and it does develop a foundation on how to communicate with a spiritual resource or should I say the traditional spiritual identity of the resource. From a practical point of view, the universe is a lot bigger than any of us realize. With such a large family of souls to watch over us doesn't it make sense there might be more than one resource to address all the spiritual supplications that might be received at any given moment? This is not to say there isn't one grand omnipresent soul able to provide oversight to legions of souls. I suspect however, a wise omnipresent soul might divvy out responsibilities to a network of capable representatives to see to the millions of solicitations potentially sent on any given day. Traditionally, many are taught from childhood to pray to one familiar source but when I am soliciting a response I summon a multitude of celestial powers from the universe I believe can assist with my request.

How you receive a response will be different for everyone. Your very personal guidance team knows you best and how you will best receive messages. You may respond best to a symbolic message. This could be an animal totem that might present as a feather, the song of a bird, or memory of a familiar melody. Some of you have olfactory responses. This ability might allow you to smell the presence of a spirit guardian. This could be the scent of perfume if your guide is female or in my case the smell of tobacco, as my dad smoked a pipe filled with cherry tobacco. Some individuals have an ability to receive a direct audible response (this is an internal communication that you know is not your own little voice talking back at you). You may have an inner feeling you could describe as a "knowing." What I call "spirit" will make repeated attempts to be sure you are receiving an answer to your inquiry.

If you are not listening to universal nudgings you might need a more significant response. This is when you might receive what I call a "spiritual smack" from the universe. Many years ago, I received one such intervention that changed my life forever. I suspect there may be times when the universe has launched one of life's curve balls and that more than likely if you are reading this material, you can affirm receiving one such encounter. It is that call from the ethers that literally says, "Can you hear me now?"

Messages can literally come from anywhere. Most of us are not going to see a Light Messenger (an angelic manifestation) materialize before us to provide an in-person response. Individually, you may also not yet be finely tuned enough to hear a precise answer. However, you might hear a faint whisper that causes you to question its authenticity or receive a "spirit wink." Spirit winks can be an unexplained knock, a light that flickers, even a light that turns on or off automatically. You might just have a spontaneous thought that pops into your head. You might hear a song that continually replays in your head that has special significance. Pay attention to the lyrics. You might glance at a picture that triggers a memory of a special loved one. Perhaps dad or mom had a favorite saying that now replays in your memory that could provide you with an answer or encouragement. A spiritual hug might come as you glance at your watch and note consecutive numbers (11:11, 3:33 etc.).

Messages might come from nature. Several books have been written regarding the meaning of animal totems. Any unusual presentation of an animal might signal a messenger. A bird might swoop down before you. I have had owls appear in my backyard during the day just to provide a significant message. Hawks, for me, also represent significant message bearers. You might see a turtle crossing a street, a dolphin breaching before you, a deer running through your yard or perhaps a fox. All present messages that might align with one of your particular queries.

While on an exploration to visit the Shaman's Cave outside of Sedona years previously, several antelope were viewed bounding over the hillside.

My Shaman Native Elder remarked he'd been coming to the site for many years and had never seen the antelope. If the presentation is unusual or infrequent, this is usually indicative of an acknowledgement or a message. Spirit knows which totem you are more likely to pay attention to or which message they are attempting to deliver. Each presentation provides a message that just might give you specific insight into a query you are seeking an answer to.

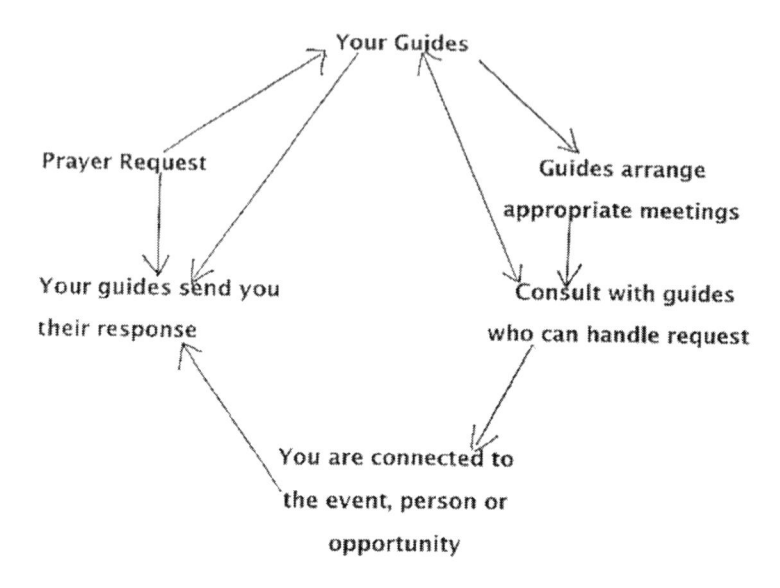

```
                         Your Guides
                        ↗         ↘
                       /           \
       Prayer Request /             \ Guides arrange
                     /               appropriate meetings
                    ↓                     ↓
        Your guides send you      Consult with guides
        their response            who can handle request
                    ↖             ↙
                      You are connected to
                      the event, person or
                      opportunity
```

The above schematic represents an elementary presentation on how a prayer request might be processed. Earlier I made a reference to spiritual resources that are invested in responding to your solicitations. First responders are most usually your personal guardians. These individuals are generally referred to as "spirit guides." When you pray or present a spiritual supplication, your prayer is intercepted by your very personal spiritual guardian network. Once a prayer request is received, it is reviewed, and your guides consult with a team of spiritual individuals who are best able to handle your request. These guides interface with your guides to arrange appropriate meetings and encounters that can best address your desire or concern. The results are forwarded to your guides and you now become connected to events, persons, or opportunities in answer to your request. Every prayer is handled in a similar fashion.

This is a simplification of a network of communication for every solicitation (or thought) you present throughout your day. The more *FEELING* you solicit with your request, combined with visualization of what you are soliciting, creates a dialogue with those guardians who monitor *EVERYTHING* in your life. If you struggle with mental visualization, looking at a picture and projecting a similar image will suffice. The universe responds to picture representations far easier than just with an assumed dialogue.

You might have noticed I refer to spiritual entities as living, conscious individuals. This is no accident. Too often we regard physical existence as the only viable experience. This couldn't be further from the truth. There is more than one life to live. In fact, life is eternal, albeit resembling varying personalities, identifying countless life experiences, and presenting in both male and female models. Those you have loved who have returned to their spiritual house are actively engaged in activity. Aunt Nellie may not be gone forever. In fact, she is probably watching over you presently. So, don't despair over the loss of your loved ones, they are quite well and actively engaged in activities of their choosing roaming freely in an atmosphere of love and creative diversity.

To reiterate, with every invocation, with every thought, a flurry of activity commences each time you meditate, pray, or send out one of your thousands of thoughts on any given day.

I always like to present a couple of examples to assist as additional teaching aides.

Example 1 - Seeking Employment:

- ➤ Say you are seeking a new job. You start musing what this job might look like.
- ➤ Start by making a list of what you are seeking. Include the salary desired (be rational). If you have no skill set as a physician, you need not apply for this position.
- ➤ Do you want to work indoors/outdoors?
- ➤ Do you want to be in an office or travel?
- ➤ Do you have a technical mind or an adventurous one?

- ➢ Do you want to work in marketing or production?
- ➢ *Do not pick a job you have no interest in*. Pick a job that piques your interest.
- ➢ Important note: If you give the universe no direction you will not experience any progression with your creativity.

In the earth's new energy paradigm, seeking something that is not in a vibrational match with you will not fulfill the lasting requirements you should be seeking. And, if you provide no details, you might not get the job you are seeking. In fact, you might receive the opposite and then ponder your misguided attempt at manifesting. Better to be detailed and precise with your solicitations.

Do not become attached to the outcome at first glance. Perhaps your first job does not check all your boxes but when you consider all potential it might just be perfect for you. Your guides are intimately aware of your personalities and always see 360 degrees while you may only see 180 degrees on your best moment of perception. In translation, this generally means you must trust your gut. This is an impeccable internal guidance system fed by your emotions.

In your job search, say you are looking for a salary of $70,000, you would like to travel (indicate the places you would like to go to), and state the type of position that fits your skillset and personality. Your guides now start researching your request. Those guides who have successfully researched your request send notification back to your guides. Your guides place a tempting thought inside your mind. You get inspired to check the internet or familiar research platforms and your eye catches interest in a particular advertisement. You start to internalize that gut instinct and you feel compelled to submit your application. While you were letting your "fingers do the walking" looking for your perfect position, your guides were busy fluttering about conducting high tech meetings with their colleagues to find those positions that might fit your perfect job.

Now comes the interesting part, how do your guides relay their findings to you? We talked about nature messages, family remembrances but there are additional ways spirit reaches out to relay messages. We also discussed listening to internal responses. But spirit is not limited to one delivery method and usually incorporates a variety of methods to be sure you are receiving the proper response. Dreams often convey information, if you can retain the information transmitted during dreamtime. If you are a vivid dreamer, you might want to record your dreamscapes through journaling. If you have trouble remembering your dreams, you can set an intention before you go to sleep that you will remember your dreams. When you awake, remember to record your nightly journey. Spirit might send a message through a stranger who overhears a conversation or a friend who delivers a significant finding. Pay attention to any sequence of synchronicities that spirit has arranged to make sure the message is delivered. And remember, within the guidelines of the current universal matrix, there are *NO* coincidences.

Example 2 - Seeking a New Residence:

The steps for solicitation will always be the same. Write down the details of your perfect place. Be specific concerning your requirements. Are you a city or a country person? Are you a single home person or a condo person? How many bedrooms are on your wish list? Include any must haves in your creative template, and include the amount of your budget along with extensive visualization.

If you are considering relocation to a different state or country start asking those important questions about, where do I want to reside? Do you like a dry climate, a cold climate or tropical one? Do you want to be at the beach or in the mountains? Start narrowing your options by the responses you get. You will want to clarify your preferences to determine what your dream residence will look like.

What does your dwelling need to have? Do you need a formal space or a modern one? If a timeline is necessary, include specific details. If you need to sell your current residence first, include the perfect price and then start clearing out unnecessary clutter from your dwelling. This is where writing down your intentions becomes helpful.

Do not assume your message will come from a familiar messenger. You may be more likely to ponder the significance of a spontaneous encounter and find an obscure message more believable. Again, the universe has eyes and ears everywhere. You might want to start keeping a journal of repetitive thoughts that seem to manifest from nowhere. Keep track of synchronicities. The more you become aware of interactive forces that seem to come from nowhere, the more you can expect synchronistic moments for you to treasure.

These are just two examples on universal/spiritual solicitations. Let's switch things a bit. What happens when collective prayers are received? The HeartMath Institute has been registering conscious thought frequencies in the atmosphere since 1991. The date was 9/11/2001. Using the Hubble satellite, the HeartMath Institute registered atmospheric emotional responses to a deadly attack on humanity that was felt around the world. The collective prayers around the world were registered atmospherically. While the results of millions of prayers may not have been harnessed instantaneously, the resultant cultural changes have been progressing ever since.

The year is 2020 and a global pandemic spread throughout the world changing lifestyles, challenging humanity, asking for global partners to unite to combat an invisible enemy. Even if you do not believe in prayer, the thoughts of humanity have been sent forth throughout universal ethers commanding action from spiritual watchers. And while I do not have access to the latest graph from the HeartMath Institute on current atmospheric thought, we are already seeing the results from our solicitations. Nations set out collectively looking for a cure. What research will reveal are multiple cures for multiple issues and a new harmonious unity worldwide.

Inspiration may have been sent to multiple individuals with the capability of supplying a resolution. One science team might receive one correct vaccination combination. Another science team might receive an extended cure for other deadly diseases. What is phenomenal is that all nations began working together for a common resolution.

When collective prayers are issued, collective resolutions can be expected. And if you look further behind an initial prayer, you will see additional miracles unfolding. What might initially seem harsh might become your greatest adventure. Yes, jobs may be on hold or even changing. Lifestyles may be challenged, but what will emerge can be a world at peace where opportunity abounds, where natural resources can be renewed, and new inventions will once again propel the world into a new era.

Listening to Guidance

What happens when that fabulous opportunity is not in your best interest? You are super excited about a new adventure. You are preparing for a grand move, a new job, a fabulous trip, or a new relationship and suddenly, things seem to be falling apart. What is going on? It is your universal guidance coming online to prevent you from making a huge mistake. Honor that you might be hung up in traffic, as this may have prevented you from being in an accident. Honor that you did not get that job because your boss might have been a nightmare. Honor that your bid for that residence you fell in love with was not accepted. You just found out the plumbing was bad. And do not spend too much time pining over your lost relationship, as it just might be protection from a future life of misery.

Pay attention to your intuition. If you are getting a feeling something is not right--honor that feeling. Perhaps your stomach does flip/flops. You might get a headache, feel slight nausea or experience an all-over uncomfortable feeling. The hair on your arms might stand on end. All these internal sensitivities are signaling something is not quite right with what you have considered your perfect pairing.

Resolving Ruffled Feathers

Sometimes conflict arises when engaging in differing relationships. I have always found it helpful to look behind the scenes to determine why conflict has arisen. Perhaps you are wondering why does dad react in a certain way. Why does mom? And this might apply to a friend, your sibling and highly likely it is a co-worker or boss. It might help to look behind the scenes to determine what is going on. If you know what the individual in question's childhood was like, this might give you some clue. If you know what a home scenario is like, this might also provide you with insight. Is a family member sick? Is there concern over budget matters? Are you experiencing the remnant from a previous unpleasant outburst? Usually, conflict is never about you but a prior encounter, an unresolved memory, an insecure feeling and much too often a fear. Take into consideration social parameters surrounding the individual's life during childhood. If you know this individual well, what were the parents like? Were they loving or strict? Did their childhood conflict spill over to the lives of their children? All factors contribute to creating conflict and what goes on behind the scenes.

The message here is that it always pays to examine what is going on that created an incident before you become entangled in conflict.

One Final Consideration

Did you ever consider what creative direction you applied to your physical being before you entered this physical existence?

Here are some thought provoking insights:

- ➢ Do you know you chose what you wanted to learn during this life? You did this to enhance your soul's awareness. This is part of your soul's aspiration and a constant desire to experience life to gain wisdom through varying life scenarios.
- ➢ What skills do you possess that have led you to your current avocation or what skill are you adding that might lead you to a new opportunity? Skillsets build on one another over your lifetimes.
- ➢ Are you aware you chose your birth family? You may have chosen your family to accelerate a talent or position as an adult.
- ➢ Perhaps your family was the vehicle that allowed you to be present at this time on earth to be the lighthouse you are merging into. You have accepted an assignment to assist in the evolution of the earth. Your purpose may be to elevate the consciousness of humanity and thus aid in creating a higher vibration in the ascension process of earth.

Reminders:

- ➤ Know all your requests are heard, none are too insignificant for solicitation.
- ➤ The more specific detail presented (along with visualization) when submitting any supplication, the greater chance you will receive the most compatible manifestation per request.
- ➤ The universe is behind your greatest successes.
- ➤ Honor divine intervention deferring to spiritual awareness for your best success.
- ➤ Watch for synchronicities; pay special attention to unsolicited information.

Ancestral Healing

Leni Morrison

IF YOU THINK ABOUT IT, NONE ENTER THIS LIFE WITHOUT AN ANCESTRAL background. Everyone on this planet has ancestors. We all carry generational heritage that is woven deeply within each strand of our DNA. When you acknowledge the lives of your kinfolk, it helps you make sense of your own blueprints. For a moment let's explore how an ancestral life can influence a present one.

An Unsolved Mystery

Most of us are familiar with the endeavors of paranormal researchers. Many investigators attempt to scientifically validate the essence of some presence lingering in homes; abandoned buildings; historic landmarks; and any areas where violence, death, and extreme trauma have occurred. No matter what is unearthed or discovered through the scientific lens, many logical or rational attempts to solve such metaphysical occurrences can never provide a doorway or a portal for the trapped soul to return home. By home, I mean the soul's spiritual dimension. Every soul enters this physical life from a spiritual house, and at the end of each soul journey, each one returns to their spiritual domain. We all have an ancient spiritual lineage, and in truth everyone has a mystical origin. And while all souls will eventually return to their transcendent birthplaces, a traumatized individual's return may take many, many years.

Some souls linger in an etheric dimension caught in an endless loop or bad memory. These "lost" souls generally remain close to the land and environment associated with their traumatic ending. Some of these "trapped" souls are unaware that they are disconnected from a physical body, and most are unaware still that all they need to do is summon spiritual intervention (a guardian angel or a deep ancestor) to assist them in crossing through the dimensional veil.

This is where ancestral healing can come into play. There is an uncanny thing about family histories: they yearn to be healed. And if a family mystery involves the emotional misunderstandings from personal tragedies, then the souls of those carrying unresolved mysteries within their DNA need to be ameliorated sooner rather than later.

Ancestral Lineage

Just for a moment consider the life of your great-grandparents, grandparents, parents, siblings, and extended family. All these entanglements can impart residual influences into your current life history. To unravel some of the lingering beliefs that may be trapping an energy in an environmental portal, try to also take into consideration the social conditions of the era.

If you have researched your family history, you may be aware of your genealogy and therefore what physical ailments you may potentially be genetically predisposed to. If you notice recurring themes and patterns that continue to replay throughout your life, this could be an indicator of a certain blueprint in your ancestral lineage. (In a future chapter we are going to investigate the age when a particular life trauma surfaced, taking into consideration the unknown factors at that specific time surrounding the insightful event.) Therefore, it is important to be aware of the defining life characteristics that may have been the social customs of the day. This awareness will greatly assist in providing any information necessary when appealing to a wayward spirit and helping the soul release from its physical boundaries.

Always ask yourself, whose life are you living? Knowledge of a family's history can greatly assist in clearing any unconscious or unresolved issues that occur in your daily life. If the soul lesson is not fully healed, continued family stress can create additional trauma further down the family line. This trauma can manifest as dis-ease or other debilitating behavioral patterns.

In my own family, sadly, my great-grandmother's body was never returned home. She developed tuberculosis in the early 1930's. The family doctor suggested to my great-grandfather that she go over to the Swiss Alps so she could benefit from the pure air. She left County Wexford around 1931 and subsequently died in November of 1932. My great-grandfather tried desperately, against all odds, to bring her remains home. But heartbreakingly, it was a near impossible feat. Her body could only be retrieved within a limited timeframe because of World War II. Because of the wretched conditions, this time frame could never be met. Sadly, despite many trips back and forth to Switzerland, none of my family has ever been able to discover what happened to her.

On a physical level, you could say it will forever remain a mystery. I know this has had an enormous impact on my own life, as often as a teenager and then later in my thirties, she would appear to me in dreams. I have since done ancestral healing with her soul and have had extraordinary confirmation of her soul's freedom through the appearance of a butterfly.

One afternoon on a winter's day, after hours of praying for her soul's release, "she" literally flew through the middle of a closed door to land on my lips as an Admiral butterfly. Any shaman will tell you this symbol heralds transformation. I knew the work on a soul level was done for my great-grandmother. That evening, in front of a roaring fire, while I was playing guitar and singing, a song for her came rushing effortlessly through the ethers and the strings. No more work was needed; my ancestor was honored, free to soar with all the other butterflies.

Creating Emotional Clearing

I hope this experience, shows you how important it is to honor your past ancestors with deep love, compassion for their suffering and absolute forgiveness. It is important to acknowledge that you are not changing the event that initiated the stress from the past; rather you are healing the emotion connected to that time. Once the emotion surrounding the event is fully cleared, the consequences for any future lineage are also cleared. You heal one family member through the realms, which allows all family members to release any residual overlays and imprints in their physical lives.

For example: The emotional toxicity of a previous lineage can be released with the expert help of a medium, shaman, healer, minister or simply by the healing power of prayer. As I pointed out earlier, this is an area I have gained much experience and insight into over the years in my own practice. Once the ancestral clearing has taken place, a genetic disposition eliminating any similar future experience with respect to that family trauma can also be finally released. It always amazes me to see how extended families respond to this healing.

Forgiveness can be understood as a moment in the present whereby toxicity and trauma from the past can finally be set free. This type of healing work allows you to create a more harmonious future without carrying the latent emotions from past generations. Forgiveness is the key to freeing both the residual energies of those who have passed before you and those still holding onto pain in the present.

Too often families carry the guilt and shame from past family events. What if your role in this life is to release and clear those past life traumas? The undertaking of this challenge can be as simple as invoking intervention from spiritual guardians or from past ancestors (if known). Solicitation should ask for release from the associated trauma or from a current scenario connected to an evolved lineage. You can acknowledge the incident but also help the residual soul to comprehend the misunderstanding by removing any emotional charge or psychic wound associated with that life drama.

When you deliberately change the thoughts surrounding the past you can massively influence the present. When you pray for the past to be healed, you completely transform the present experience. By changing the present, you therefore alter your current and future lives. This is referred to as quantum consciousness, understanding that all timelines co-exist in the present, the eternal *Now*.

Here is a simple reference that can help to explain this quantum ideation. Consider there are multiple channels available on a radio. All channels exist simultaneously. One channel can be dialed in at any given moment, but changing the channel allows access to a different frequency. This is similar to accessing quantum fields. Quantum fields exist simultaneously with each corresponding to a different frequency; the higher the frequency, the higher the reality.

The Power of Prayer

Stress in the family line can create separation from a sovereign source, especially when love has been denied. Separation from Source can lead to unresolved generational patterns in the future if left unresolved. Through acknowledgment, understanding and forgiveness it is possible to heal any family crisis from the past. When you can release the past with love, you free future family lineages from engaging in intergenerational trauma.

Life experiences can thus become teaching elements for the soul. If a chosen lesson is ignored, the lesson repeats, each time presenting with greater intensity until the lesson has been fully realized. Many challenges can be imposed when hidden vows, curses, or karmic issues from a past life are unresolved.

In an effort to clear compromising life patterns and emotional challenges, I conduct interdimensional sessions with my clients. Through 'opening up' the presenting soul-picture and allowing higher guidance to flow through, I can engage with ancestors who step forward to assist in clearing past traumas, imposed injustices and pain. I am always in awe at how quickly past grievances, anger, and repressed feelings are lifted through prayer, invocation, divine intervention, and an openness to release surfacing issues with love, meditation and a soul language of codes and symbols. The resultant response is a greater sense of freedom and renewal. The power of heart-centered-prayer can never be underestimated when clearing generational imprints. So, if you are feeling the burden of family overlays, perhaps today is the day to release the past with love. You may simply ask yourself, if not now, then when?

Jilliana Raymond

Suicide

I want to address the topic of suicide. Many religions disavow a soul that has ended their life prematurely. Too often this stigma shrouds a family with the shame and guilt associated with the accumulative events that may have led to the individual's inability to cope with presenting life issues. More than likely the soul carrying this ancestral scenario is attempting to clear something from a "soul family" perspective. (We'll discuss soul families in a future chapter.) From a spiritual perspective this has *NO* bearing on the record of the soul, nor from the perspective of the parental family, or from the viewpoint of any associated individual emotionally attached to the individual.

In my family's history there have been four suicides during this lifetime. This unfortunate history provides me with many significant details I need to be aware of. First, I carry the family scenario of premature death through suicide. This means I must be mindful of the predisposition so when emotional compromising situations present themselves, I must dig deeply into my own psychic composition to overcome the scenario of a premature departure. Secondly, I need to honor the lives of those who found the only solution to their internal suffering was to find a way to end their mental anguish through suicide. I can appeal to the higher consciousness of the individuals, acknowledging the difficulties each encountered, provide them with a deeper understanding of the life lesson they chose to overcome, and remind each they are divinely loved. I ask each what is necessary from their mental perspective to help them release the trauma they have endured. This releases the scenario from occurring in future lineages. In essence, those family members who chose to embody the lesson of suicide carry a high vibrational frequency to be confident enough to want to physically absolve the experiential scenario on behalf of their soul family. Only a master would choose to explore this challenging emotional life compromise. Presenting and reminding the individual embroiled with the emotion of failure, the non-acceptance that their life mission was to overcome the emotional negativity of this scenario, and then remind them of their master status is usually all that is necessary to release the compounding trauma.

Usually, if a soul has prematurely exited before mastering a soul lesson, they return to the physical dimension bolstered by countless years of star-lit guidance with greater determination to overcome the challenges that may present. Once again to be clear, there is no condemnation from a spiritual perspective for any soul that has prematurely departed. While that soul may need to re-enter a physical domain to overcome the life scenario, there is no shame or failure label associated with the initial traumatizing event.

One final note on the subject is that while sorrow may linger for the grieving family members still exploring the physical realm of learning, their family member is renewing their spirit. The burdens and challenges of their life may have become too compromising to master. The renewed soul will return with more determination and greater resilience to overcome future challenges.

Soul Assignments

Leni has been talking about family healing and how this could contribute to your present journey. Kryon (an angelic group whose assignment is to coordinate earth magnetics) says that as you continue to raise energy frequencies, you can alter your DNA. From my point of thinking—with the current infusion of higher energy frequencies beaming towards earth from the sun and other universal frequencies-- the ability to alter or embellish DNA sequencing is possible. It does take mastery of re-patterning subconscious patterns to successfully accomplish this. Once harnessing reprogramming of frequencies occurs though, anything can change.

Some years ago, one of my soul assignments was to participate in healing the land--specifically surrounding battlefields. At that time, I resided in the Washington, DC suburbs and had access to many battlefields, including the Civil War Battlefields of Manassas, Antietam, and Gettysburg. I also lived near the colonial battlefields around Williamsburg, Jamestown, and the Rappahannock regions where early settlers were caught in conflict with Native American tribesmen.

Those who live in battle-scarred regions know that the energies from ancient battles can linger on the lands for centuries, especially after a particularly volatile engagement. Ireland has seen many ancient conflicts, as has much of Europe. In fact, much of the world has known conflict at one time or another on some level. Those tasked with healing the land become gateways, (portals or vortices) that allow souls trapped in a volatile timeline to transition back to the spiritual domain.

I will try to paint you a picture of what this might look like or how it looked to me. Early 2000 I lived on the outskirts of the Manassas Battlefields. An ancillary resident in my home was a Civil War Union Major. His presence brought me comfort, as I considered him a protective resource, especially doing soul crossing work.

Walks through the Manassas National Park would produce a volley of experiences. In certain high drama locations, I would see a creek turn red with blood. I could see confederate and union soldiers pointing muskets at close proximity at one another. I could smell the musket fire and hear the boisterous charges of the soldiers in conflict. One home on the battlefield outskirts became a field hospital. This site was located at a major juncture that crossed through the battlefield. Each day as I drove to my office, I could see the wounded laid out on the lawn. I had to convince a Union surgeon guarding the wounded I was there to help the injured return home. It took nearly two years to complete the soul crossings here.

On another adventure, a day trip to Gettysburg would invoke a different experience. The Gettysburg conflict was a particularly bloody engagement. Twenty thousand soldiers died in one day's fighting. The fields today still cannot be plowed because of the number of bones strewn across miles of battle lines. To commemorate the soldiers, monuments were erected to honor the fallen providing their names and battle regiments the soldiers fought in. The monuments now hold the energies of many of the soldiers still trapped in time. One of my assignments was to see if I could free those trapped. This did not come without complications. A good friend accompanied another minister and me on that day. My friend unfortunately experienced a total personality change because of the energy she absorbed during this outing. Confused over the day's events, she would understandably defer from any further adventures of this nature.

My guides would often remind me I needed to clean my house (my physical body) to eliminate the resistant residual energies of those soldiers not ready to leave the timeline they were locked within. The residual energies from an ancestral soul can leave behind side effects that can linger for weeks. By the way, I should extend a disclaimer at this moment that those performing soul release work should have some formal training in the endeavor. This work is not meant to be performed by anyone not pursuing a "soul calling."

It did not matter how many angels I called in, it seemed that familiar family members were better at convincing the lingering soldiers that their families had long departed. The ancestral family could be very persuasive in coaxing their departed loved ones to join them. I remember one evening returning home from one of the soul transfer engagements to find my house glowing silver and gold. This was interpreted as a thank you from the numerous soldiers' 'soul lights' who were released from their timelines.

I am pleased to say that after repeated attempts to release trapped souls from multiple battlefields, the residual energies have largely returned to their spiritual homes. Even at Auschwitz, the many prayer groups that have come to the historic site have done much to transmute the energies of this devastating conflict. While the historic site is still extremely difficult to visit, much of the residual energy of the tortured souls has been released. While visiting one of the barracks where the workers were housed in unbelievable inhumane conditions, pictures were hung on the wall of that unit's residents. I reached out to one of the souls and asked if there were any remaining there. Her response was that none of them ever wished to return there in a physical embodiment or in a spiritual one.

Each time you send forth a focused thought/blessing to honor those who have fallen, you transmute the energy of that location. Every step you take with your higher frequencies is healing the land. Do you see how important your energies are now?

Chance Encounter?

I had just returned from my European tour. I had heard from three independent sources that I needed to attend a Kryon conference being held that year in Cancun. I had little intention on going, one because I would be traveling alone, two because it was an expensive trip and three; I have followed Kryon for nearly twenty-five years and familiar with most of the presentations. Included in the conference agenda were some phenomenal presenters and after all, three trusted consultants urged me to consider going. That has never happened before. Leni and I have told you to look for synchronicities as affirmation you are listening to higher guidance. I try to listen to spiritual direction, so I booked my trip.

Single conference attendees were encouraged to search for someone to share a room to defer costs. You know how that goes, I really was not sure how sharing a room would work but at a cost of $400 per night and a five-day conference, I was highly motivated to find a roommate. Since I was late to register for the conference, roommate selection was limited. But one individual stood out and responded to my inquiry.

Leni had received a similar spirit nudge and she too was looking for a roommate. Leni would arrive the day the conference started. I told her I would be wearing white slacks and a zebra top and added she could not miss me. And she didn't. Our initial meeting was as if we had known each other for ages. Conference attendees remarked how much we would miss each other when the conference was over. (If they only knew.) Some months later both of us realized the only reason either of us attended the conference was to meet each other. What if spirit knew all along that our meeting would lead to us teaching a series of webinars and writing this book of knowledge?

Both of us come from differing yet complimentary backgrounds. Leni is Irish born while I am American born. Both of us are involved in healing endeavors. Leni is a galactic shaman capable of clearing ancestral energies as well as being a healing practitioner. I am a spiritual teacher, spiritual life consultant, energy channel, and alternative therapy instructor/practitioner. Both of us have years of accumulative spiritual training and have similarly conducted years of research into the complimentary practices we present. Both of us are committed to assisting a global band of "light weavers." Both of us know the individuals who seek our specialized intervention will become a powerful group of "light weavers" who will in turn take what they learn from our teachings and pass it on to others. This is part of our soul assignments as we have both agreed to be in service to a galactic light force.

How will all this awareness affect real change in your life? How will it change the life of another? Leni and I both play instrumental roles in the vibrational healing of our clients and the earth. We are both sharing our stories to help others explore their own source light and make this life as meaningful as possible. It is important to be cognizant of the ways your spiritual alliance integrates in your life to provide you with information and interactions to allow you to capitalize on the greatest opportunities possible.

Meditation - Ancestral Healing

Leni Morrison

During this meditation, using focused energy and spiritual guidance will help you let go and clear lower ancestral energetics associated with painful familial stories.

Find a quiet space. Provide soothing background music if you like and prepare to go into deep meditation. You should be able to feel the energy infusion, even if you are reading this information, by placing your intention behind releasing the residual energies from a lingering past. If you prefer, you can record this meditation to listen to it time and again. You might even consider presenting this meditation to a group of friends and taking turns reciting the meditation to others.

Begin clearing by taking three deep breaths, breathing in through your nose and expelling your breath through your mouth. With each breath you will find you are going deeper into a reflective space. With every breath you will relax deeper. Outside noise or distractions will fade away.

Call in the four healing angels. (It is not necessary to know their names.) Your intention will be all that is necessary to summon them. Call in St. Germain and the angels of the violet ray.

Call in the higher consciousness of your mother and ancestral grandmothers. State inwardly that you have called in their energies to release anything that does not represent a loving bond between you. Ask to increase the light between you. If you sense any unwanted connection, use a sword of light to disconnect an unwanted tether.

Ask that any contract, agreement, or vow of suffering be released and incinerated through fire. Your higher consciousness will now clear your Akashic record (soul record) needing to be released from your maternal line.

Call upon Metatron (God's messenger on earth). Metatron will guide you to the healing golden temple of light. If any maternal ancestor steps forward, ask that any unwanted connection be released or any difficult past encounters be forgiven in love. If you are able, look for any earthbound soul trapped within the bloodline and release these energies as well. Ask that these souls be greeted by their guides so they may be released back to the multiverse.

Become aware of your energy body noticing if there are any lower frequency memories, energies or cords still lingering. Call in Archangel Michael to cut any remaining cords and sever any energetic connection to this pattern *NOW*. Ask your higher consciousness to make this pattern change.

Hand over your ancestral lineage to your spirit guides. See all past traumas now being destroyed in the violet fires. If there are any residual promises, agreements or vows you no longer wish to maintain, rip them up and throw them into the violet flame. Clear all lives, all dimensions and collapse all timelines that represent any conflict with your maternal ancestral lineage.

Now ask for an empowered healing symbol from your ancestors to replace this old ancestral conflict. This could be a flower or crystal. Allow this symbol to dissolve into your DNA to provide remembrance and eternal healing throughout your physical body. If you feel the need to speak to your mother, here is an opportunity to do so. You may say anything without any concern for retaliation. Clear the maternal ancestral line completely.

Now call in the ancestral father lineage. State that you have called in the higher consciousness of your father's ancestral lineage to increase the light between you. Notice any unwanted cords or threads linking your energies together.

Call upon Archangel Michael's sword of light to break any contracts, agreements, or vows of suffering to be disconnected and throw these into the violet flame. Ask for clearing from the ancestral father line through the Akashic Records. Release any trapped emotions related to your father's ancestral lineage including any judgements or karma. Feel extended light coming into you now representing the cleared energy fields.

Notice any residual energy fields that linger representing unresolved family trauma. Ask now that these traumas be healed and released with love and forgiveness. Ask that your higher consciousness fills you with love, harmony, compassion, understanding, and release you from all fabric of traumatic consciousness.

When you feel your tasks complete, take a deep clearing breath thanking your ancestors for coming forward and your spiritual guardianship for assisting in releasing any tethering to any ancestral lineage. Feel refreshed, energized with a renewed spirit. Feel empowered and renewed as you walk forward upon your life journey.

Non-Conflict Resolution

Jilliana Raymond

Every layer of wisdom is taking you on a different journey designed to help you release conflict and imbedded emotions that may still be compromising your life. I'm going to take you on a non-invasive confrontational journey to resolve conflict. I developed this protocol because of my own aversion to conflict. Most individuals who have implemented this powerful life tool have found amazing resolution to their personal conflict. Combine this technique with the powerful meditation Leni is presenting and you will experience personal transformation.

We can learn much from native tradition. Native Americans knew about the ancient energy of the land and its sacred vortices. They also knew about the importance of self-reflection held within the sacred space of the medicine wheel. While visiting Sedona, Arizona I commissioned a Native American shaman elder to lead me to a sacred site on a local Indian reservation called the Shaman's Cave. The journey is not for the average individual. We drove miles through the wilderness only to hike several more miles through the hot desert, climbing through the arroyos to reach the mountain top. Throughout my encounter the elder taught me about the wisdom in the land. He looked deep into my soul to extract some revealing insight on relationship restrictions and core issues I thought I had already dealt with. These issues were compromising how I envisioned my living world. He told me of the significance of the medicine wheel. He informed me how individual power is amplified within this sacred space.

Leni Morrison and Jilliana Raymond

Before the Meditation

The following non-conflict protocol was born from the wisdom gleaned from my Native American explorations. There are a few directions to follow creating your personal sacred space:

1. Nothing negative can enter your sacred space.

2. Within your circle you can resolve any personal conflict.

3. You can initiate communication with those who have offended you. These might include a co-worker or a boss you are having some difficulty with. You can call in a friend you are having any difficulty with. You might call in a romantic partner. You can resolve conflict with a mother/father, sibling or extended family relative. You can communicate with loved ones in spirit. You can plan future creative adventures. You can accelerate personal healing and carry-on soul-searching communication with your creative source.

4. No one may enter this sacred space unless you have issued a personal invitation. You will be communicating with the higher consciousness of the individual(s) you have summoned into your sacred circle. If you have multiple concerns with multiple individuals, it may be best to invite one individual at a time to be sure you are totally focused on communication with that individual.

5. You may enter your sacred space as often as you like. The individual(s) summoned must respond even if they are reluctant. Notice the body language or facial expression of the summoned individual. This will tell you much about the personality and mood of the individual. The individual must remain present until you have dismissed them.

6. You can direct whether you wish to engage in conversation with the individual or if you just need for them to listen. In this case, they may not speak.

Once you have completed your communication, you will ask the individual to exit your sacred circle. Again, pay attention to the body language as your solicited individual exits your sacred space.

You can anticipate resolution shortly. Your guardians and those guardians of the individual you communicate with will begin to provide insight to both of you. This will ultimately lead to resolution of your conflict.

Your sacred space can be anywhere that speaks to you. Determine if your energy is most complimented at the beach, the desert, the forest, or the mountains. You can surround this space with personalized elements that have special meaning for you. My space is a crystal temple in a tropical environment where birds sing and wildlife flourishes. A gentle waterfall tumbles into a nearby pond. This is my spiritual residence when I am not on a physical world.

Embellish your visualization with the sights, sounds, and scents of nature. Smell the pine of the forest, hear the gurgling of a creek, hear the birds calling in the forest, and feel a gentle wind caressing your face. If you're at the ocean, smell the salt spray and hear the tumbling of the waves.

When you select your sacred site, you will create a complete circle. This can be done with stones, crystals, pinecones if your location is in the forest, shells if you are at the beach or flowers if you are in a meadow. Place some organic material around the circle that designates your sacred space. You will be sitting in the center of this space. Create a visual object to sit upon in the center of your circle.

Leni Morrison and Jilliana Raymond

Note the picture of a labyrinth. Just like the medicine wheel, labyrinths were established to provide inner reflection while walking the path of an intricate pattern. Changing directions could address the four directions of spiritual influence or it could represent the release of a particularly troubling thought. Entering the center of the labyrinth would reflect completion of the meditative projection and exiting the labyrinth would symbolize the resolution.

Discovering Your Mastery

As an example, I have chosen a forest location to begin this exercise. You may have already determined who you wish to invite into your sacred space for this exercise. You can yell at them, you can get emotional, you can tell them exactly how you feel and relate to them how much they have hurt you. The idea is to release some suppressed emotion you felt you could not communicate in a physical encounter.

Non-Conflict Meditation

Jilliana Raymond

Close your eyes, get comfortable and begin to relax. Take three slow deep breaths.

You are in a field of daisies. The sun warmly shines down and there are no clouds in the beautiful blue sky. There is a gentle breeze that moves the daisies to and fro. Up ahead you notice the forest edge. At the edge of the forest, you notice a path. You feel compelled to explore where this path leads. As you enter the forest you hear the gurgling brook off to your right. The birds are singing and flying excitedly through the trees. The air is fresh and there is a gentle breeze that washes over your face. You can smell the pine boughs as the air feels fresher than you can recall.

As you look further down the path you notice a bright light shining down from the sky. You continue to follow the path and move closer towards the cathedral light. You notice a clearing where this light has been shining through the forest canopy. There is a perfect ring of stones within this space, and you notice a log in the center that beckons you to come and sit for a while.

Something has been troubling you and you are having conflict with an individual you would like to resolve. If you feel the need, you can call in your spiritual guardians to be present within your sacred space.

Once you have settled into your sacred space, you are ready to initiate an invitation to the individual(s) you wish to share in your communication.

> Your solicitation could begin something like this: *I, <u>(state your name)</u>, invite the Creator of all that is, my spiritual guardians and the higher soul of <u>(name the individual you wish to call into the circle)</u> to enter my Sacred Circle.*

A log now appears on the outer rim of your sacred circle. You ask the higher consciousness of the individual you wish to communicate with to join you in your sacred circle. You motion for them to take a seat on the log. When both of you have settled you can begin your conversation. (Allow several minutes of reflection here to be thorough).

Find a place to end your conversation. You now become aware of a bridge that crosses the brook to a path on the other side of the forest. Thank the individual for entering your sacred circle. Now motion for the individual to exit your circle. Observe them as they move towards a bridge that crosses the brook. As you watch the individual cross the bridge you notice them turn, as if to ponder the discussion and potential resolution. You watch as they disappear down the forest path.

If you asked your guardians to be present, thank them now for coming as well. You feel much lighter now as you stand to exit your sacred circle. You start down the path you entered the forest on but stop momentarily to ponder your recent experience and wonder if your sacred circle is still there. The cathedral light is still shining. As you continue down your path the birds are chirping even louder. The gentle breeze again brushes against your face and whistles through the pines bringing fresh air to your senses.

As you reach the forest edge you look out upon the field of daisies. There is a renewed spring to your step, a youthful feeling of joy and freedom as you find yourself skipping through the field. The sun's warmth bathes you as you contemplate your accomplishment.

Take another deep breath in through your nose and release the breath out through your mouth. When you are ready open your eyes, feeling totally renewed and energized.

You can return here anytime you wish. You can resolve countless scenarios in your sacred space. You can receive information from your guides, your family in spirit, you could ask for a raise from your employer, or you could envision your future. Hopefully, you know how powerful this energy tool will be for you. It is amazingly effective.

Power of Your Word

Leni Morrison

So that all the stars align for you in truly magical ways, practice kick starting your day using heart centered affirmations. When you lovingly inform your universe about how wonderful your day has been before you even get out of bed, you are transmitting a vibration of absolute faith. This powerful signal aids you in matching the higher realities always available to you in any one moment. When you step into your power and state with absolute knowingness that things are happening *for* you instead of *to* you, more abundance and infinite possibilities also start flowing in your direction. A magnetically charged affirmation may be something like "*just for today I choose happiness,*" or "*just for today I will focus on gratitude.*" How about "*just for today I will make all those around me smile.*" Perhaps you could be the alchemist of your day and channel that wave of pure excitement by stating something like "*Today I am expecting some magic from my universe!*" or "*Thank you for surprising me with something utterly magnificent.*" The Law of Gratitude promises multiplied and accelerated experiences when pure gratitude is expressed before any evidence has actually materialized. Always bear in mind, before you conjure any decree, your words must connect to your heart so they are amplified with love. Your affirmations should also be personalized so that they have true meaning for you. Always endeavor to use your own words and not those from another. The words of others will not carry the same light codes as those evoked from your own core being.

The Use of Affirmations

Your words, when used consciously, have the power to transform everything for your highest happiness. When you accept that *you* are the creator of your day, then every previous moment has the added possibility of unfolding in spellbinding perfection.

Ghandi said:

- Your beliefs become your thoughts.
- Your thoughts become your words.
- Your words become your actions.
- Your actions become your habits.
- Your habits become your values.
- Your values become your destiny.

Harness the energy behind inspiring moments and uplifting feelings so you can allow them to manifest new opportunities for you. Create affirmations that represent accomplishments, desires, and goals. When you are fully present, use your affirmations to mindfully acknowledge you are in fact *living* your desired goals. The more you give thanks to your universe, the more you will amplify the promptness and continuation of future manifestations. The momentum builds once you keep acknowledging the power behind the thoughts. Affirmations can therefore be thought of as manifestation tools. Affirmations not only promote inner confidence but they also send out a clarion call to universal guardians to assist you with your heartfelt requests. Always remember that your universe is constantly working *for* you.

Once you have cleared all your negative belief patterning, including programs of lack, the actual *having* of your desires gets a lot easier.

If your initial affirmation does not yield your perceived vision, it is always best to defer to universal wisdom rather than become disheartened. Remember, that which manifests on your behalf is *always* going to be heart aligned. That which does not manifest comes from the ego's design. It would be wise to differentiate between the two. Always ask for manifestations from an open loving heart. Be sure to acknowledge Mother Earth with a blessing too. This will amplify the manifestation.

Once your manifestation is received, thank your universe for complying with your request and add to your gratitude a solicitation to provide you with more opportunities. A great one to use on receiving a manifestation is *"thank you, bring me more."* Remember it's only human constraints that limit your thinking surrounding personal manifestations.

When you share gratitude with spiritual allies, you are sending a message to your universe of your balanced contentment and positive reflection. If you change your response around what is happening outside of you, you subsequently change how you feel internally. You can achieve this by using thought and conscious language to mindfully redirect uncomplimentary issues. It is far more desirable to act from a state of acceptance, surrender and love. This field of energy is referred to as the *"zero point."* The transformational healing benefits that are available to you once you employ this more playful approach to life are innumerable.

Please be mindful that if you are using self-limiting language created by a false belief system you have either learned or created out of pain or fear, you may be placing limitations upon your ability to achieve life-long aspirations. The list of self-sabotage can be endless when you are focused on limitation and not expressing confidence in achieving your potential.

Once you realize *you are the master of your reality,* no one else can drive your car. When creating affirmations, try choosing your words with the same exactness you would apply to picking out a diamond ring. Using this level of precision and awareness, you then infuse the feelings behind those words with raw authenticity and pure focus. Your thoughts, when channeled in the direction of self-love, can completely change your destiny. You alone hold the keys to your happiness. Ask yourself, is *Now* the time to get busy creating more abundance, happiness, and oceans of love?

Leni Morrison and Jilliana Raymond

The Power of Language

Just as we can use language to uplift and inspire, we can also use language to unhinge another's life. Let me share with you the power of words through two short stories.

Scenario 1: A Deadly Disclosure

Years ago I was teaching in Greece. One day I noticed one of my students was incredibly sad. I spoke to her to see what was going on. She told me her grandfather just died. She was distraught, as she believed he had many more years to live. She went on to explain that for years her grandfather had lung cancer, but the family decided it was best not to tell him. Instead, they would maintain his health with medicine and intermittent check-ups. His doctors were all advised not to disclose his condition, and none were to ever let him know of his diagnosis. Then one fateful day, a new uninformed doctor came into his room. The physician looked at his chart and declared 'I see you have stage IV cancer". Her grandfather died that same day. The impact surrounding the word 'cancer' was the catalyst that led to his death.

Scenario 2: From Hero to Zero

My aunt is a nurse in a busy Dublin hospital. She remembers the day a patient bounded into the doctor's office for his routine check-up. He was feeling fantastic as he floated through the reception area and down the corridors, greeting all the nurses warmly with a big smile and cheery hello. Once in the office he was told his cancer markers were clear and he was given a clean bill of health. Absolutely overcome by the shock of his hitherto undisclosed diagnosis, he hobbled out of the office an old man full of the worry and fears surrounding his diagnosis.

I believe it is incumbent upon all physicians and people with whom we have placed our trust in to have a deeper understanding of the power of their words. Regarding illness, the words of a disease or virus alone have the power to change a life. Wisdom, compassion, and loving care must be employed when communicating a diagnosis.

Power of the Shadow Controllers (Media)

How many times are we disempowered by media channels presenting the latest sensationalistic broadcasting? The repetitive bombardment filters through fragile senses often creating a sensation of fear. This ultimately distracts us from our spiritual practice. Even those souls who consciously create worlds of cheerful reflection and transmission can at times be leveled to dismay when listening to sensational broadcasts. Time and again we can become saddened by world accounts of disharmony or dive into depression over the latest heartbreaking headline. No matter how much we set our days up for perfection, anyone of us, at any moment, can be pulled into the fray by such news bulletins. The best way to insulate yourself from the darker infusions of toxic or painful information overload is to simply express deep compassion for all those involved and invite in spiritual guidance to resolve the situation. Then balance your fractured energy field with some positive influence. Go outside and shake off the news. As best you can, move into a state of happiness immediately. I find jumping helps to shift emotional states quickly. Find your own release and use that method.

Another great way to deal with harsh news broadcasts is to make the disciplined step to limit your news exposure. Negative news can be addictive. Notice if you have an addiction to join suffering by over-watching sensationalistic news. After years of being involved in teaching political science, I became so polarized and opinionated, I felt so sad and powerless all the time. The day I took all the news apps off my phone was the day I began to return to a much happier state of being (which, by the way, is my natural state of being as it should be yours too). It wasn't so much that I was bypassing the political storms and world chaos more than it was sheer soul-preservation. Now I try to do a minimum of three minutes of world news a day. I find this is sufficient to be kept in a relative loop.

Maybe you too could remove a few apps that are toxic for your body and well-being.

Just as you exercise your body, you must also exercise your mind to build up immunity to lower thought forms brought about by the language you have become exposed to. All of us have, at one stage or another, have felt the poisonous effects of words when directed towards us in anger and thoughtlessness. It is often hard to take back those toxic exclamations, even when they have been launched in haste. Language expressed in an angry moment can leave lasting effects on energy systems throughout a lifetime. Every thought and word carries vibrations so powerful that the harmonics of each syllable can create an energy that can change the outcome of a situation dramatically. Words are indeed magic. Words possess such power they can cast spells. If you didn't already know, this is where the word *SPELLing* comes from. Be sure to cast good spells by choosing your words wisely. Always understand that the energy, emotion, and intention placed behind words are extremely potent.

Self-Destruction

It's time to start to realize that your body is always listening to your every thought. If you attack your body with raucous criticism, your body will respond accordingly to the energy your message is sending. You never want to deface your physical appearance by declaring how you hate being overweight, or remark how displeased you are with your hair, or remark that your teeth are crooked etc. It is kinder and wiser to turn the negative reflection into a positive affirmation. You know just how hurtful it can be when someone you love and trust scolds you or tells you how disappointed they may be with you. It is wise to remember these strident statements are actually the insecure projections of the sender. Statements that reflect displeasure towards another generally have nothing to do with you at all but *everything* to do with the sender. We all hold mirrors up to the world. It is quite understandable that people only see themselves in you. It makes me think of the famous adage "What other people think of me is none of my business." One of the highest places you can get to is being independent of the good opinions of other people. Words to live by. Thank you Dr. Wayne Dyer.

When it's Not Possible to Walk Away

Whenever possible, walk away from people that cause your heart to close. Just notice how the words others speak make you *FEEL*. If you feel good, stay. If your heart constricts or your stomach tightens, walk away as fast as you can.

When it is not possible to distance yourself from individuals whose energy is steeped in negative conflict such as an employer, family member, significant other or other influential individuals in your life, try this experiment. If they are invading your space and using heavy, dark language that contaminates your energy field or lowers your vibration, inwardly envision a shield of platinum white light all around you and breathe into this field. Then think of peaceful, melodic, blissful words that generate inner calm. Try to reflect on thoughts of grace, serenity, love, and harmony. Allow the energy of those words to soothe your frenzied mind. Begin to radiate the energetics of words representative of a harmonic vibration. If you can calm yourself enough to do this with every breath, you will begin to relax. It is always better not to engage in conflict, and it is always best never to respond to those who would attempt to assault you verbally.

On a final note: practice word alchemy. There is always a better way to say something. Try to be conscious of words that carry a higher vibration. If you consciously adjust your vocabulary so your words dissolve and diffuse all negativity, it will become easier for you to navigate your day in the most phenomenal ways. With over 750,000 words in the English language why choose words that perpetuate pain and sadness? Go and make your day magical.

Jilliana Raymond

What you are discovering is that language is not just an audible communication. The spoken word becomes an event in motion. I'm passionate about teaching and demonstrating how the power of thought and energy in our language directly impacts the life you experience. I can think of no better way to demonstrate the power of language than to present you with the results of an experiment conducted by Dr. Masara Emoto, a Japanese educator and scientist. Dr. Masara Emoto wrote several books on his experimental discoveries with water. One of his books--*Messages in Water*, documents Dr. Emoto's experiments conducted on jars of water.

To begin his experiments Dr. Emoto exposed various written expressions affixed to jars of water. One set of beakers received toxic expressions. Another set received uplifting, loving expressions. Dr. Emoto instructed his students to express audible language to the beakers. The group receiving the written negative expressions would receive harsh language and the group receiving written praise would now receive language of loving praise. In addition, Dr. Emoto exposed one set of beakers to loud abrasive sound and the other to soothing melodic sounds.

At the conclusion of a twenty-one-day period Dr. Emoto photographed frozen sections of the water from each of the experimental containers. Water from beakers receiving positive projections produced purified water crystals. Water taken from the containers receiving negative frequencies produced distorted, incompletely formed crystals, the quality of which mimicked the appearance of cancer cells. Pictures of his resultant experiments are depicted within his work *Messages in Water*.

If spoken or written words can have this impact on water, imagine how words impact the events in our lives and on one another? Add the power of emotion, amplified by the intensity of a delivered word, and the power unleashed can inspire or destroy any projected target.

To further prove Dr. Emoto's hypothesis on the power of audible words, he took his experiments to polluted reservoirs in Japan to see if his classroom experiments could change a large body of water. He invited community

Discovering Your Mastery

participation, instructing observers to project loving expressions towards a noted body of polluted water. With media cameras rolling he took comparison water samples. He first took samples from the polluted water. As expected, the water samples revealed the broken cellular structure of the polluted water crystal. Then following the loving audible expressions directed towards the water from the community, he collected samples of the transformed water. The conclusion of the community experiment revealed the previously known and proven pollution of the chosen site had been converted into a purified body of water.

What can be learned from Dr. Emoto's experiments? Imagine what a difference projected words could make when directed towards polluted bodies of water in local communities? For that matter, what actions do you think loving transformational thought projected towards the earth and her resources could provide? What happens when our thoughts/words are applied to the human body? If an expression of love can change the shape of a water crystal (and consider the human body is approximately 70% water), what effect do you think thought and word frequencies might have on human cells? Or for that matter what effect do you think sound and accompanying intonation directed at a specific object might create? If sound can alter the composition of a water crystal, imagine how sound could also change the composition of a cellular structure, on our environment or even throughout the world.

What effect do you think soothing music piped into hospital rooms might provide? Do you think there would be fewer traumas during surgical procedures if pleasing sound is included during an operation? Do you think sound could speed the healing process of traumatized cells or provide support to sensitive emotional systems? The answer to all these considerations is a resounding *"yes!"*

Would it surprise you to know that an individual in a coma can hear words and conversations conducted with such an individual? There are countless patient cases where individuals have awoken from their coma to recount the messages delivered and conversations held while they were seemingly unconscious.

Words that carry the greatest potency are those dressed in the deepest compassion and love. Conversely, those words drenched in anger, hatred, fear, and retribution carry the weakest vibration. It is advantageous to maintain a higher life vibration by using heartfelt words of compassion, understanding, harmony and love. When our frequencies are lowered by projecting negative thought and expressing toxic language, we are exposed to viruses, bacteria, and invite the unpleasantries of our projected thinking to return to us on waves of unwanted manifestations accelerated by our lowered vibration.

Of course, it's not just words that contribute to our energetic reserves but the combination of words, their structured messages, and the intention we place behind the delivered communication that determines the promptness of our manifestation. We have all said things in haste. We have all forgotten there are better ways to express our feelings. The next time you find yourself in an awkward encounter where verbiage becomes toxic; you might consider putting the individual in a box of mirrors. I have done this on many occasions. This is a highly effective "light" tool and not one to be unleashed before careful consideration of the effects that will be felt by the individual you are encasing in the mirror labyrinth. This prompts me to present you with this consideration; all are accountable for their actions through spiritual eyes.

Technique:

Simply visualize the individual encased within a box of mirrors where all sides, top-to-bottom, side-to-side, front-to-back, are mirrors. No matter which direction the individual turns they will see their own reflection--the one that is not very pleasing.

Another great tool to employ when you are surrounded in a negative environment is to continue to surround the individual in blankets of pink light representing loving energy. See this in waves of energy descending over this individual. It may take several minutes for the energy to dissipate but a love vibration will eventually transmute most negativity.

Discovering Your Mastery

Usually, when someone launches a banter of negativity, it has nothing to do with you. It is often a case of your being in the wrong place at the wrong time where you become the closest energy to receive the uncontained emotional expression. Too often those we care for the most become targets of uncontained emotions. These expressions come from some limitation the sender has yet to process. It is unfortunate that those receiving the ill-thought unexpected harshness must process the unwanted emotion.

Words, sounds and thoughts are not just inanimate expressions. They are living frequencies that carry emotional imprints that register within our energy bodies. Choose your words wisely and remember it is always better to present positive intention. The power of thought can change outcomes, renew a planet, change the direction of a storm, generate rain, heal a body, and change the world we live in.

Meditation - Power of Your Word

Leni Morrison

All meditations begin by finding a calm space, perhaps lighting a candle or playing soothing background music. Three clearing breaths usually allow the body and mind to relax ready to receive messages of light. To begin, take three deep breaths in through your nose, releasing the energy by blowing it out through your mouth.

> Call in Archangels Michael, Raphael, Gabriel and Metatron. Call in your personal guardians.

> Call in all you ever were, are and ever will be. Feel your full presence coming into this moment, now.

> Breathe in love, light from the higher dimensions and begin to feel the power of universal energies surround you.

> Begin to open up all your chakras in diamond light. See radiant sparkles of diamonds along with a star-filled array of light frequencies encompassing all of you.

> Say inwardly—"In my throat I activate the full resonance of my voice. I have a voice that needs to be heard. I am authentic. I live with integrity. I communicate my thoughts and feelings easily. I share my wisdom and insights with others. I am truth."

> Now recite--"I Am a *Free SOUL* and I activate the full power and resonance of my being through my word. I am choosing to utilize impeccable words immersed in love. I am a vast being of light, not limited by time, space or language. My words create magic and this magic expands beyond all limits."

> Say inwardly-"I Am a beautiful being. I understand the power of my words. In this time of ascension, I rise above all chaos caused by another's

misunderstanding. I surround myself with those individuals reflective of my positive outlook. I no longer choose to be immersed in any energy representing limitation or suffering."

> Inwardly acknowledge–"I Am a happy vibrant soul. I reclaim my power and I reclaim my light. I am done with all limitations from my past. I can see that my words are keys to my freedom. Just as my thoughts become my words and my words become my actions, I am choosing to write a powerful and brilliant script now. I understand all limits are an illusion. I am recalling my true nature to be happy and at peace. My very essence is light as I expand into spaciousness of my connection to All That Is. With every breath I remember my actions become my habits, my habits become my values and my values become my destiny."

> Acknowledge inwardly–"I choose words that empower me. I allow the light and the magic of my words to uplift all those around me. I ask my Higher Self and all higher guardians of light, known and unknown to me, to assist in further anchoring my connection to the light through my careful choice of words. As a free soul I ask for a divine dispensation to release anything in my energy fields that is no longer complimentary to my divine essence to be removed. I ask that all false belief systems be transmuted. I ask that I am now cleared from using any lower frequency language in all directions of time."

> Acknowledge—"I Am a person of my word. I use clear communication skills and freedom of expression. I Am Light, I Am Love, I Am Freedom. My words are reflectors of my light. Every word I speak is infused with the light and love from my soul. All my beliefs are being upgraded in light of love and therefore all of my language reflects this enhancement. My heart and mind are a reflection of my words and actions that are in alignment with love. I dissolve all old limiting agreements and rules I have self-imposed that no longer complimentary my new energy."

> And so it is!

Learning to Love Yourself

Jilliana Raymond

"You may have all the faith needed to move mountains, but if I have not love, I am nothing." 1 Corinthians 13:2

IF YOU ARE LIKE MOST OF US, TOO OFTEN WE SEE OUR FLAWS AND FORGET to reflect on our perfection. This chapter is all about *Love*. Therefore, loving what might be considered a flaw is your perfection. This is an opportunity to reflect upon what love is, why love is so important and how to incorporate more of the inner qualities of love into your life. Perhaps I can influence a self-review by reminding you of who you really are. The above reference to Corinthians provides you with a glimpse into your magnificence--and your fragility.

Most of us have faced life challenges--challenges that perhaps became the catalyst for exploration into your spiritual essence, provided you with an opportunity to explore a soul calling or launch a lifetime agenda that will lead to deep passion. Long before you became a physical being, you answered a clarion call that went throughout the universe. The invitation came from Source (another name for a Divine omnipresent energy) asking for the greatest angels in the universe to assist with the evolution of humanity. The solicitation further indicated you would face many challenges, perhaps a war, endure a pandemic that would paralyze the world, and rewrite history for eternity. In addition, stipulations went on to advise you that you, more than likely, would not remember who you were and that personal sacrifice might be part of your physical journey. And yet you said unequivocally *YES*—Yes, I will come and I will do my part. And here you are; the greatest angels in the universe on assignment to accomplish an almost impossible task. The task is to increase the frequency of the earth, to enhance the vibrational essence of humanity, and bring Gaia (the earth) back to the universal jewel she was always intended to be. More importantly, you faced an almost insurmountable task to anchor harmony, peace, and love throughout the earth. You did this so all could experience equality, opportunity, and abundance. But in the process, you may have forgotten to *LOVE YOURSELF*.

I want to remind you of your essence, your perfection, to play a little with you—to remind you that you are never alone and that the vibrational frequency you carry has forever changed the world and the universe.

The Universal Matrix is built on two main principles:

Love and Light

All universal energies are variations of these principles.

What is Love?

Love originates in the heart of God. In its purest essence, it is not judgmental, carries no bias, is never shameful and never blames. Love inspires and sees the potential in all things. You are a particle of divine expression and as such—*PERFECT* just as you are.

Let us look at some descriptions of love.

- ➢ Love is understanding and tolerant; yet guiding by its example.
- ➢ Love is totally unconditional and never vindictive.
- ➢ Love knows all emotional trauma, all fears, and knows all pain.
- ➢ Love is strong. It becomes the teacher that holds steadfast throughout adversity. It does not enable but inspires. It sees all purposes and all lessons as perfection.

- ➤ The heart of God does not recognize one characteristic, one life experience, one appearance, one life position, or one ideation as better than any other.
- ➤ Love knows all contributing circumstances that can diminish an ability to love unconditionally.
- ➤ God's love has no timeline, no boundary or limitation. God is love and love is all there is.

Loving Yourself

How often do you take time to love yourself? In life we can become so preoccupied in daily activities that we can lose awareness of all that you contribute to the lives of those around you. Too often we tend to devalue our roles in our families and disregard how we may have influenced the lives of our friends and those whom we encounter. Our work is often unappreciated. We forget that we are an integral part of a complex tapestry of life. I want you to understand that I am including myself in the messages I am delivering. The point is that our lives matter. What we do, what we say, how we play, how we love, and how we are loved matters.

To love unconditionally is to love yourself first. For without internal love, we are less likely to be able to express love externally to those we encounter. When we splinter our energy in the pursuit of assisting others without nurturing ourselves, we exhaust our own energy systems.

Self-love is an initiative to examine those characteristics that may be out of balance. Your task is to learn to identify those areas of weakness, adjust the imbalance as you are best capable of doing, and honor those characteristics that are uniquely yours.

The patterns of your early childhood can begin to establish what contributes to your belief systems and largely determines how you interface with your surroundings. If childhood memories are conditioned in Love, then your reflection can view challenging encounters as surmountable, where personal growth attainable and where life potential abounds. On the other hand, if your early memories are dressed in limitation, fear, or anger, this complicates your ability to maintain optimism. Your energy will become laced with doubt, an inability to experience life without challenge, and a round robin recurrence of unfortunate events.

Here is another wonderful statement from Corinthians:

> *"Know thyself, and to thine own self be true."*

If you can learn to become more content with your own design, you can learn to become more accepting of all neighbors and their varying differences. Take time to honor yourself. Do something for yourself that makes you feel special. When you feel self-worth, others will recognize that quality within you. Love begins within you, then radiates outward. When you love yourself, others are attracted to the reflection of your vibration.

Nurturing Your Inner Love Core

Most of us fall short in the self-love category. We distract addressing self-love issues by enlisting some of the following life actions:

- Do you have difficulty saying "No?" Ask if while being of service to others, are you honoring your own needs?
- Do you have an overwhelming "to do" list?
- Are you throwing yourself into your work, neglecting time to nurture yourself?
- Do you feel imperfect, carrying the guilt of some imposed emotion launched towards you from another?

It is imperative to release the toxic components of the unwarranted labels that represent the tonnage of old baggage imposed upon you from others. These can be childhood tapes that continually play out in your mind-- Mom always said,--Dad always said. These tapes generally represent the limitations of the sender and do not represent your authentic essence. The opinions of others intended to limit and minimize who you are do not represent your highest perfection. These thought limitations need to be eliminated.

Emotionally charged impressions imposed upon you from others are not representative of your light. There is a wonderful statement that declares: "never give your power away." I want to add to this concept by stating "never give your light away."

In a future chapter we are going to discover your inner joy guide. This internal guide is your inner child. Everyone has an inner child no matter how old or who you are. And the truth is your inner child is calling the shots. A happy inner child equals a happy life. Your job is to identify first how to communicate with this energy and secondly determine what it is you need to do to bring balance into the inner consciousness of your inner child.

Too often we ignore our inner child putting off "play time" for something far less exciting. He/she can literally present you with opportunities you never thought possible. To begin to reacquaint you with your internal guidance system, I would like to introduce you to some nurturing energies to apply that can help to reverse some less than optimal habitual habits you more than likely have unknowingly adopted. It is said it takes twenty-one days to create a habit. Here are some suggestions to begin to implement to establish new lifestyle patterns:

- Call in spiritual assistance to help you accomplish your "To Do" list.
- Treat yourself to a massage, pedicure, or ice cream cone.
- Take a walk or run before your busy day. Do so without any guilt.
- Make a golf date, beach day, or hiking adventure.
- Take time to read that book you just cannot put down.
- Schedule a shopping event or night out.
- It is okay to indulge in a special treat. It will give you more enthusiasm to reinitiate your healthy dietary lifestyle.

Say you are a little overwhelmed with the daily routines that seem to have no end. Call in a spiritual guardian to help you accomplish your overwhelming to do list. You will find that "To Do" list will melt quickly when you ask for help.

Say you spontaneously get a craving to do something special, something perhaps out of character, but something that will make you feel good. This might be a massage, a pedicure, or just indulgence in an ice cream cone. If a spontaneous thought pops in your mind and presents an energized feeling, follow-up on it.

You have a busy day, but you are reading a great book and just want to see what Chapter 5 has to say in that book you can't put down. It cannot take that long to indulge in that chapter, and it will be so delicious to read about that exciting character. Whatever you felt you would not accomplish because of your indulgence, you complete with ease.

Schedule that special event, a golf game, a shopping event, a weekend get-a-way--anything to lift your spirit. You might take a drive in the country or sip a cup of espresso at a local café. You ponder whether you have the time but make the commitment to nurture your inner feelings. You now find you have much more energy to accomplish your tasks.

You have been dieting but a friend encourages you to go out to lunch. The menu has some decadent offerings that you cannot resist. You are feeling a little guilty for the caloric intake. But that super satisfying indulgence gives you enough resolve to continue your new healthy lifestyle.

The point is that it is okay to indulge. And you have more than likely proven that by doing so you can accomplish twice as much with more determination to accomplish a special goal. Your momentary indulgence reveals to the universe that you are willing to cultivate self-love and thus responds in kind with your new energized spirit.

It is not selfish to say "No" when someone asks you to do something you really aren't excited about. You might launch more self-regret not honoring the ability to say "no," than giving into the pressure of those fulfilling their own agendas.

Here's What Love Can Do

- ➢ A smile can brighten another's day. Your loving expression may just have been the tonic that made the difference in the individual's life providing them with a self-reflection of worth.

- ➢ Love can settle any conflict.
- ➢ Love can heal a heart.
- ➢ Love can provide inspiration to another who has lost their way.
- ➢ Love can launch a meaningful project that can change the world.
- ➢ Love and its confidence can calm a storm.

Remember, how you glow internally is how your Light is registered externally. Now is the time to honor YOU, to nourish and regenerate so you can emerge stronger, more capable to handle your new position, accomplish your goals, inspire another, and emerge as the empowered angel to live your life in Love. Love really is all there is!

Meditation - Learning to Love Yourself

Leni Morrison

Take three clearing breaths, each time breathing in love. Hold the thought of love. With every exhale, release all that is not love. With each breath find yourself relaxing deeper. Outside noises or distractions disappear as you reflect on your inner consciousness.

> Call in all your guides, helpers, teams, star councils or any spiritual guardian currently working with you. See a column of white light now descending into your crown. This is the white light of ascension.
>
> Open your heart to receive rainbow diamond light to enhance your heart energy.
>
> Turn to the four directions, calling in the angelic symbols from the North, South, East, and West.
>
> From the North visualize Archangel Uriel holding a wand of rubies.
>
> From the South visualize Archangel Michael holding a sapphire sword.
>
> From the East, visualize Archangel Raphael carrying the Emerald crystal wand.
>
> From the West, visualize Archangel Gabriel carrying a platinum chalice.
>
> Call in Quan Yin. She tells you now that you will receive a healing and an upgrade to embody the deepest connection

towards self-love. Let go of all resistance to allowing self-love to embody you now.

Say inwardly: I hold myself with great tenderness. I am becoming whole in my relationship to myself and others. I am worthy of great compassion and willing to receive unconditional karuna compassion from my higher self now from this moment forward.

By the power of my I AM presence, it is commanded that this activation of the resurrection codes within my DNA is accomplished in this moment, Now.

By the power of my I AM presence, it is commanded that my awareness be filled by my own Divine love and compassion in every present moment.

I trust myself to incorporate this energy, I am emotionally safe. I understand that from this foundation of self-love, comes a stronger initiation into greater depths of compassion available to me as a Christed being. Those embodying the "Christ Light" are carrying the highest vibrational frequency currently present on earth. This photon light is like the Mahatma Light of India.

Command the karuna compassion to heal your heart now.

Honor yourself with deep compassion. Hold and love all parts of yourself throughout every present moment and in every circumstance. When you accomplish this your heart will soften. Accept the gift of karuna compassion as the standard you deserve. Let go of the need for another's approval. You only need permission from yourself to experience deep compassion.

Affirmation:

I am present within my authentic experience. I vow to treat myself with kindness in every way. This is my new being.

I understand that karuna compassion takes my awareness directly to the root belief systems of my original wounds.

I AM choosing now through my higher awakened self to use the magic of this compassion to release the places within me that feel abandoned and unloved.

I am willing to love what in the past seemed unlovable, unforgiveable or lacking within me. I now give myself permission to release myself from the bondage of old belief systems that has caused density and prevented me from receiving light and healing.

I call in my inner child now. Your inner child speaks from your heart acting as your guardian angel, allowing you to bestow self-love upon yourself.

I now integrate this full initiation of karuna compassion throughout my entire body on all levels of my being.

It is done.

It is done.

It is done.

I am now free to love myself at the deepest level. I now know and accept myself as pure love.

What Makes You Who You Are?

Jilliana Raymond

I HOPE BY NOW YOU ARE AWARE THERE IS MUCH MORE THAN ONE LIFE TO live. More than likely you have had multiple earth incarnations. None reading this material are young souls. In fact, most are such old souls you have been part of an ascension team for millennia. Some may have traveled back from the future some three hundred years.

What past life experiences might be contributing to your current life assignment? Everything you surround yourself with reminds you of some aspect of a past life. Look around your residence. What artwork signals your heritage? What lands do you most want to visit? What foods do you like to eat? All these items remind you of some familiarity to your past.

If you ever watched a Star Wars movie or became a Star Trek fan, then you can easily see how planetary explorations can take you to other star dimensions. While you may have a predominant planet of origin, it is likely your soul expertise was gathered from multiple planetary systems over lifetimes.

With the presentation of earth's evolutionary history there is a greater importance why the "family of light" has returned to be here now. You are part of a growing "Light" community of the world to be the cosmic glue that unites worlds. There is a biblical reference that God sent his *Only* son to earth to experience the physical suffering of earth's inhabitants. Jesus (Yeshua) came to teach humanity that all are sons and daughters of one Great Light. Just like Jesus was the envoy for humanity so many years ago, God has sent many sons and daughters to assist with earth's ascension and the inhabitants upon her into higher dimensions within the galaxy. All are particles of the Great Is—God particles of that Great Light. With earth's ascension, many planetary systems will evolve and raise their evolutionary frequencies as well. This is why so many planetary systems are invested in the earth at this time. Their evolution is inherently entangled to the earth's ascension.

With your new awareness you carry more light. When you carry more light, those you encounter, and your surrounding environment benefit from the light infusion you leave behind with every step you take and every encounter on your path. When your soul radiates love, this causes a planetary regenesis. When you work with the light, you can unlock your own Akash (your personal soul record) and remember more of who you are and the importance of your mission.

Who Are You?

In previous chapters you were given hints of your magnificence. I have found over the many years of my research that any time I can discover another piece of my composition it provides a better comprehension of who I am. Through this work I hope I can provide you with a better picture of your entire essence or at least open your curiosity so you will want to explore a little more of your composition, those past, present and even future adventures.

I wonder if you ever considered the possibility that your origin might begin on another planetary system. Some information might seem beyond comprehension but just for exploration fun consider for a moment if this could be plausible. If you are open to a concept that your origin might be from another advanced civilization in the universe you might find exploration through *YouTube* to be a wonderful resource. Consider the following signs that might indicate your planetary heritage.

Discovering Your Mastery

Signs You Are a Star Energy

- You answered the call of Light.
- At times you can be fatigued, feel pressure from the energies around you.
- You felt unique as a child, perhaps you felt aloof, or that you did not "fit in."
- You may have had or continue to have paranormal experiences.
- You are empathic.
- Your body functions differently reacting more intensely to pharmaceutical intervention.
- You may note a variety of allergic symptoms to a variety of products that are synthetic or enhanced.
- You are highly intelligent, if not scholastic.
- Your body's limitations are frustrating to you because you remember you can fly.
- Your dream life is vivid.
- Others are often aware of your energy and this can be intimidating to others.
- You are telepathic and may be aware of another's thoughts.
- Babies are drawn to your energy.
- Often being in a large crowd is uncomfortable for you.
- You are overly sensitive to energy.
- People seek your energy, especially strangers.

Everyone is on an evolutionary soul journey. This is in addition to your agreement to assist in the earth's evolution. Many teachers (and you) have endured many challenges, just as the master teachers before you. Just think about this for a moment. Each time you overcome one presenting challenge it accelerates your evolution into higher dimensions. Whether you are aware of your "light assignment" or not, you designed specific challenges to add to the acceleration of your soul's agenda. You (and your subconscious) are on a path designed to provide you with the experience and knowledge to accomplish your unique soul's path.

Do You Know Why You Chose Your Birth Parents?

First, I do hope you know you were solely responsible for choosing the individuals who would represent your parents during this lifetime and that your choice was not some random encounter. This does not mean all parental relationships have been "Father Knows Best," or that some relationships might be contentious. But for whatever reason you made an agreement with the individuals who are (or were) your parents during this life incarnation. Here are some of the reasons you made your specific choice:

- ➢ Your parental choice provided you with a vehicle to enter earth's atmosphere, just to be here during this time for earth's evolutionary acceleration.
- ➢ Your parental choice would provide you with some physical trait to allow you to enact a specific goal.
- ➢ Your parental choice will teach you a specific lesson that would enhance your soul's evolution or provide you with the experience to become a teacher for another.

If your life endeavor is to pursue a specific life achievement or life exploration, you may have chosen parents who already had a foundation in the pursuits of your choosing. If your life goal is to teach, perhaps your parents were educators. Perhaps your family alignment will provide you with a financial head start to help you accomplish a pre-determined business adventure. If your life goal is to design a specific invention, provide a cure for disease, or accelerate a designed field of research, your DNA may have been infused with the DNA of your parents to assist in accomplishing your life goals. Say you want to play a specific sport and your parent is a recognized athlete. Your parents might pass on genetic characteristics to provide you with features that would support your career goals.

I am going to assume that while you may have played some sport or became your class queen or king, your prime objective was not due to your momentary life detour. In fact, your adventurous escapade could just be an interim experience while waiting for the appropriate moment to accelerate your universal endeavors. It's almost as if there is an internal clock keeping time on the events in your life. Think of this internal synchronicity as the activation of a subconscious program that becomes activated at a precise moment on your physical journey.

Sacred Contracts by Carolyn Myss

Several years ago, Carolyn Myss wrote a marvelous guide that categorized the *Sacred Contracts* every individual engages in to assimilate some important quality that you designed to experience while you were in spirit. At your soul's direction you deemed this specific scenario advantageous for your soul's growth. Ms. Myss categorizes every individual into eight specific archetypes. She then breaks down the archetypes to align with individual life expressions. Her work is worth exploring if you are interested in discovering more of your life design.

Jovian Archive, Ra Uru Hu

Another human researcher, Ra Uru Hu (Jovian Archive), received channeled information providing insight into the human mandala based upon personal birth dating. You can acquire your personal mandala by going to *jovianarchive.com* and provide the required birth information. This, by the way, is a free offering. The sample mandala will demonstrate a model of an individual who is a manifesting generator.

The Human Design program delineates how you interact with those you encounter by determining which of your chakra gateways are open or closed. Extensive study of this system provides insight on how you interact with individuals. The study of the mandala system takes years to master. Should you desire a more complete interpretation of your individual mandala, the Jovian Archive can connect you to individuals capable of interpreting your specific mandala.

If you look at the sample mandala, note the white boxes. These represent open circuits. The sacral chakra depicted in this sample if visualized in color would be red. Red boxes represent closed circuits. In this mandala the second chakra is compromised. This indicates potential conflict with individuals who also have a compromised second chakra. Meeting an individual with an open chakra will provide the missing link to open this chakra center and connect with individuals who are more compatible to your specific energy frequency. The black bars represent blocked channels.

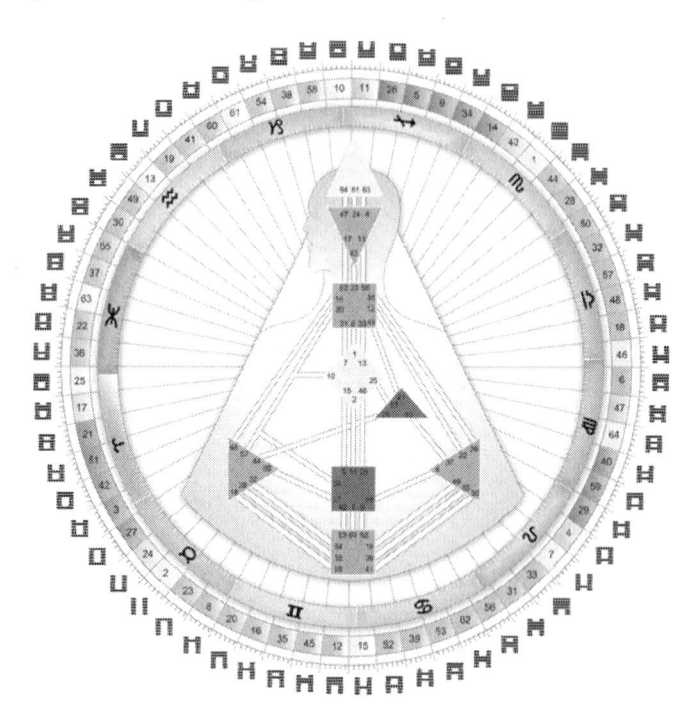

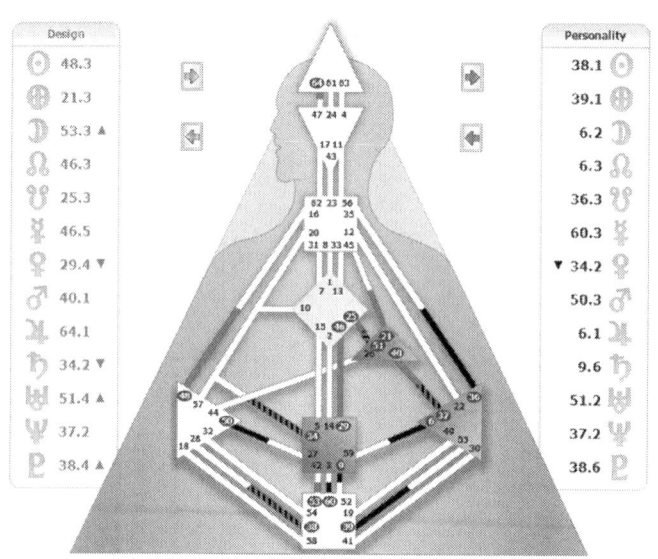

Discovering Your Mastery

Every human mandala is categorized into five specific models. Character modules include the manifestor, the projector, the reflector, the manifesting-generator, and the generator. This individual generally functions with a "can do" response when invited to participate with individuals or events.

The Life You Were Born to Live by Dan Millman

Another fabulous compilation in discovering your life purpose and human design is a book written by author Dan Millman: *The Life You Were Born to Live*. This work uses your birth date to provide you with your potential life characteristics.

Example:

To begin, take your birth date (say 2-26-1942). Add the numbers together 2+26+1942 = 26; then add the 2+6 = 8. Your birth number would be 26/8. You will then refer to the guide within *The Life You Were Born to Live* to determine your life purpose. The numbers represent birth characteristics that will most likely be an accurate representation of your specific characteristics. In the case of the above example, the 8 = Abundance and Power. The 2 = Cooperation and Balance, and the 6 = Vision and Acceptance.

With this example you can now ponder the basic traits that begin to present your life picture and help you understand the differing scenarios that provide the foundation for your life on this journey.

Why Did You Choose Your Body Type?

During my research I found it fascinating that you are the designer of your body type. I never thought life experiences could be so complete as to decide which frame, gender or physical appearance could be decided upon and that these choices were not some random assignment.

Some individuals will choose a body that is predisposed to illness. You might wonder why anyone would choose such a dire experience. This advanced choice is made by a master soul desiring to acquire the experience this scenario will provide to help another with a similar life affliction. It is likely the aspiration of this soul is either to become a medical resource or to become a future spirit guide for a pending soul. It takes many accumulative life experiences before a soul is given the assignment to be an individual's soul guide. The guide must have direct experience with every potential encounter or challenge the physical soul will experience during one lifetime.

Another explanation would include an individual exploring medical sciences. This individual will take the comprehensive information back to their spiritual residence to begin to explore curative resolutions for individuals that would be afflicted with a presenting illness or dysfunctional compromising disease.

Your desire might be to become an athlete. You would want a physique compatible with your particular athletic endeavor. A husky body type might be predisposed to contact sports. A lean physique might become a runner, swimmer or bicyclist. If your desire would be to become active in the modeling world your outward appearance would be important. Your DNA structure would need to take on the glamorous attributes of your physical desire.

If your endeavors include the mental acuity of a scientist, inventor, problem solver, engineer, you'd want to include components to include a sharp mind, some serious imagination and the passion to explore.

If your pursuits lie with the arts, you might have chosen body features that would complement this scenario. You might need a keen eye for color and form if your artistic expressions on a particular art medium. You might have fine acuity for musical creations, a melodic voice, an ability to write a song or conduct a concerto. The point is that the body characteristics you choose represent some physical ability suitable for the life you desire to experience or the goals you wish to accomplish.

The following questions might also present you with some considerations to ponder:

> You chose whether you would be female or male. Gender roles are important when considering a specific life design.
> You want to work outdoors. Perhaps you will be creative in conservation, environmental studies, biologic exploration in the sciences, exploring life-enhancing compounds, discovering new species of life or protecting earth resources. What body structure will support your creative designs?
> Here is a difficult scenario. You want to experience the life of an individual with a physical challenge. Perhaps in a previous life a beloved individual suffered from genetic compromise, illness or physical impairment and your desire is to discover a cure or coping modality to allow an individual to experience life fully. Too often the destructive forces from war leave individuals without limbs. Several years ago, replacement limbs were only an experimental ideation. Today artificial limbs allow mobility and some normalcy following a traumatized experience.

I've pondered how one goes about choosing the varying qualities and characteristics that make up one's human design. I am not quite sure if you go into some body room and just like a forensic artist start to assemble body parts. Nevertheless, your physical design isn't accidental. This is just another amazing part of a soul's amazing physical journey.

Is a Past Life Training Assisting You Now?

Had you considered that a past life experience might be contributing to your current life? We are Masters and you didn't evolve to be on planet earth now without many life experiences that have become part of your legacy. Check out the work of Brian Weiss in his book *Many Lives, Many Masters*. Dr. Weiss documented countless client scenarios where past life experiences were directly contributing to some current life obstacle. Uncovering the experience connected to the current life allowed the individual to clear the emotional attachment and release the memory of the prior life attachment.

Perhaps the best way to get you thinking how a past life has contributed to the one you are living now is to tell you about some of my past life experiences.

While training has provided much of the knowledge I embody in this life, it is my supposition that past training has aided in my current life pursuits. I am also quite certain that your collective lives have represented many differing scenarios. Your roles will have included wondrous journeys, as well as those you would rather forget. You have been masters for many of your lives but all in all you have accumulated wisdom throughout your varying encounters to become the individual representation of who you are today.

Some thirty years ago I embarked upon an explorative journey into a more complete awareness of my physical and spiritual composition. The catalyst that initiated this exploration was a desire to understand why I attracted difficult life challenges. Perhaps like you now, my initial research was not always in alignment with my fundamental life understanding. I grew up within a religious framework with life circumstances exposed to the traditional protocols of cultural and society expectations of the current time. Those earlier beliefs did not seem to coincide with the research I was pursuing but the discoveries were irrefutable. I was emerging a more confident, understanding, and wise individual within my evolving world.

A few examples of the lives that most likely contribute to what I present today are a life as a scribe where I was tasked with the documentation of significant texts. Today I am an author. Writing comes easy to me, but if someone told me thirty years ago, I would become an author I would have said emphatically this wouldn't be possible.

In addition to my writing skills, I have studied healing arts. In fact, I have explored multiple modalities for nearly thirty years. My healing practice accelerated many years ago when I studied with a mystic--a man of exceptional healing ability. I watched this man perform serious miracles. He could repair a broken back, remove cancers, realign frozen shoulders, lengthen legs--and yes--even part water. As it turns out I had a previous lifetime with this healer. It is this past connection I utilize to assist in my therapeutic practice today.

Remembering Your Past Lives

What clues do you think might provide a memory of your past? Most of us have a unique trait, passion, natural ability, desire to travel to specific places, or we might surround our décor with specific items that tell us of some past journey. To help you investigate some prior life and for your consideration:

- What literature are you drawn to?
- Why did you choose a specific piece of art?
- What type of art are you drawn to?
- Do you have artistic talents?
- What colors are you attracted to?
- What places are you drawn to? Is it the sea, the desert, the mountains, or tropical forest?
- How do you feel about Britain, Ireland, Greece, Mexico, places in the US? Are you drawn to the southwest, mid-west, northeast, or west?
- If you have a desire to travel, where do you want to go?
- And--if you have been to a specific destination did it bring back any memory or did you get an uncomfortable feeling about being in that location?
- Do you have a food preference? This will delineate a country heritage. You might be fond of Asian cooking or drawn to South American foods. Perhaps your palate salivates for Mediterranean foods or your sweet tooth remembers French culinary delights.
- Does history fascinate you?
- What history era is most interesting? Is your fascination from a specific conquest? Your interests here will provide clues to at least one past life experience.
- Does investigative service, military service, fire service intrigue you?
- Are you drawn to caregiving, healing modalities, nurturing endeavors, or perhaps teaching roles? These all indicate a piece of your individual life puzzle.
- Does your interest lie in archeology, research, humanitarian causes, or discovery adventures?

➤ What things do you dislike? These are just as important. It will be helpful to make a list here as these clues can be specifically insightful.

All of these considerations may contribute to some past life awareness. Resistance to a country or scenario might signal some less than desirable life encounter.

> **Example**: I have no desire to visit France. This is interesting as there is a direct family connection to Alsace Lorraine. However, I am aware of a significant tragic life experience that ended in France during a religious campaign. It is obvious that the memory of that life journey continues to play a role in this lifetime.

What do you think your greatest encounters to date are that have contributed to this life? How do you think these are contributing to your current life expression? You really have little idea who you are but perhaps you are getting a glimpse into the ingredients that contribute to who you are today.

What Makes You Who You Are

Leni Morrison

THIS IS A MOMENTOUS TIME FOR OUR BEAUTIFUL PLANET. JUST AS ascending Gaia is receiving massive influxes of photonic light from above and crystalline energies from within, so too are the souls roaming around this giant blue pearl.

The aspiration held within these pages is for you to not only trust the higher guidance coming from your own spiritual teams and ancestors, but also to open up to your own *Avataric* soul aspects (from the Hindu tradition meaning a divine teacher in a physical form) and *Monadic* soul aspects (in Greek tradition meaning over-soul). In this time of great awakening, we are all being asked to dive deeply into inner realms and reflect on 'Who do you think you are and ask am I actually multidimensional'? This involves being aware of your full *I AM* presence. This is the full acknowledgement of all that you are now, all that you ever were and all you will ever be, and all this in one moment of time.

When creation first started, the first humans or humanoids were created in the same likeness as the universe. They held within them many layers, levels and dimensions. These beings also held within their twelve strands of DNA the very same light as is held both within the higher dimensional realms of creation and within illumined beings (like the Seraphim, the Ascended Masters, as well the Supreme Creator so many call God).

This light from God, or the Creator being, infuses all other planetary systems through our solar systems and the star gate of the sun. This light moves into your DNA through toroidal fields in your energy body and then upgrades all your energy systems, as well as Gaia's. This diamond light connects the ascension bound in unity intelligence that binds us all together as One. One could ponder then, that if the universe does actually exist within you, and you are in fact made from star dust, then perhaps all must begin to accept that all dimensions exist inside you too.

When the human element starts to see that all are 'star energies' or 'children of the stars,' then you start to see your role in the world very differently indeed.

Many star children are now being called to remember their origins and their divine birthright. As humanity experiences a massive awakening or shift of consciousness on earth, never have so many beings experienced such a stirring in their souls to know or demand the truth. This is called the "quickening." This could be likened to a set of unique instructions or codes activating inside each soul. This is helping each to remember their mission on earth. The entire soul template is coming into balance, harmonizing and activating equilibrium in the physical body. Now the radiance of the soul is literally shining through the physical form. People are actually radiating (glowing) this light. This forward progression, with regard to the soul's evolution, began to accelerate in the year 2017. Those awakened souls or light workers on the forefront of embodying their roles during the ascension process have been accelerating since 2011 or before.

Most on earth already carry some galactic coding within their DNA. As your vibration changes through personal research (reading advanced materials, attending workshops, meditation, etc.) you evolve spiritually, consciously activating *Christ Consciousness* (the highest state of spiritual consciousness) within your DNA. You begin to access higher cosmic and divine gifts and develop stronger connections to your angelic, elemental and avatar aspects.

It is wise to note that being an embodied human is incredible. It does not make any individual lesser or in any way inferior to our cosmic cousins. We in fact carry multiple strands of both galactic and human DNA. We therefore have the ability to receive more spiritual gifts, advanced emotional intelligence and more magic in our lives than we ever could imagine. Once all can tap into their royal heritage, we will create boundless miracles on earth. Life will be even more extraordinary.

I hope you are starting to see that being 'awake' (fully aware of an ascension shift) on earth at this time is *powerful beyond words*. In fact, many beings from our galactic universe are literally queuing from the milky way to observe Gaia through the ascension process. This is why so many advanced souls are returning to experience life on earth during this pivotal point in her evolution. It is such a triumph when humanity can step into their sovereignty and master individual free will to make choices that are heart aligned embracing love and light.

As stated earlier, we have been receiving photonic light upgrades, new earth crystalline infusions, as well as living light codes and light language into our DNA since 2011. This light-work helps those 'awakened' to move the planet out of third dimensional energy and assist Gaia greatly with her ascension. Star children, by just simply emitting their light, greatly assist in advancing the human genome. This invisible language of codes and Christ Consciousness activates the dormant DNA within others and helps them to remember their origins.

This chapter would not be complete without a reference to the individual known as Jesus. "Christ consciousness" was seeded on the earth through the love of Jesus. It was through *His* benevolent, compassionate presence that the seeds of unity, forgiveness, love and peace were planted into the souls of humans. The awakened contingency of humanity is once again activating their twelve-strand DNA to embody their connection to the Christ conscious field. This is referred to as the Golden Era. This divine calling is now waking up all the souls on earth, allowing them to step into their light. Individually, you may even feel like you are in an electromagnetic gateway. This is largely because you are tapping into the electromagnetic field of the earth at an atomic particle level.

On a final note, it is very important that you understand that the frequency you are vibrating at changes the frequency of all those around you. Your vibration activates those around you in a field of diamond light that is filled with love and its expansiveness. Harmony and unity consciousness opens the hearts of all humanity and accelerates soul wisdom while assisting with the soul's ascension.

Life from a Higher Perspective

Jilliana Raymond

This chapter represents another powerful lesson in understanding how universal design functions helping you to understand your individual roles and how you are making a difference because of the part you are playing to add to universal wisdom throughout the galaxies.

The following insight represents another important component to understanding life elements. It is said that those who overcome a lesson become the masters who present life teachings to one another. Hence, the title of this chapter—*Life from a Higher Perspective*. I am going to present you with some scenarios representing potential life challenges to allow you to think how you would react to a specific challenge. At the very least the information might provide you with the rationale to understand the challenge you might be experiencing.

What if you are extensions of the work Jesus (Yeshua) performed so many years ago? What if each of you came to earth to experience the human condition from your personal perspective? Each of you present valuable information that you are continuously sending into the galactic ethers to report on the conditions of life on earth, all while learning how to master specific lessons you and your soul designed specifically for you. Why is the accumulative information essential? Very simply, the answer is to enhance your personal soul's evolution. The more advanced answer is to provide this world's living matrix an amplified experience to assist in accelerating universal dimensions. You provide these wisdoms through every challenge you have ever faced and overcome. You are the living masters on this world now. And more than likely, you are the living masters of your galactic community. You have made many sacrifices to be here now. All eyes from a grand universal audience gaze upon your accomplishments and your hardships. Your watchful guardians acknowledge that the journey is not always easy.

There have been times in my life when I did not think I could take one more step. In fact, every great master that has entered a physical world has endured many challenges. Every one of them experienced great doubt. They may have momentarily lost their faith, no matter how spiritually oriented they may have been. And they may have called for assistance from a higher source on multiple occasions only to have been reminded that they were never alone and often supported with Divine intervention.

You will never know the courage it takes for someone to overcome one obstacle or what defines another's limit. All individuals are unique, learning to cope with adversity in whatever means is compatible with the way that individual's coping mechanism works. Through the courage to overcome your challenge you are teaching another by your resilience and providing comfort for another who has momentarily lost their way.

No one can truly know what choices any of us will make when faced with an assortment of life challenges. You could theorize how you may react when faced with any life alteration, but unless you have direct experience with a presenting challenge you may not be able to adequately access the knowledge or support required to provide a solution for another. It would be wiser to reserve criticism regarding another's life without fully comprehending the complications of that individual's unique challenge. Those who have direct experience with difficult life scenarios become the best advisors to help guide those who are or will experience a similar incident.

Discovering Your Mastery

Divine Intervention

What if your challenge is divine intervention, designed to steer you to a different path of awareness? Consider some of these trials. Just for a moment place your awareness in another's challenge. Imagine what emotion the journeyer might be experiencing. Consider some of the challenges and potential reactions. Then consider what changes could be undertaken to minimize the experience as if you were walking in their shoes.

Body Compromise: What if you are the soul who has chosen to experience life with any difficult body compromise? This might include blindness, autism, deafness, a crippling handicap, Down's syndrome or include any physical distortion such as a cleft lip, limb discrepancy, facial/body anomaly, scoliosis or many other physical compromising scenarios. The emotional compromise these conditions can create can last a lifetime. What courage would you draw from? How do you believe you would conduct your life or engage with others? Just for a moment place yourself in one of these examples and ponder how you would react.

Dangerous Occupations: There are many categories that fit into this challenge. Soldiers enrolled in military missions face unknown encounters on a daily basis. At a moment's notice they must remain ready to respond to an encroaching threat. Many have witnessed atrocities most individuals may never know unless involved in a territory where the conflict of war is a life expectancy. Upon returning from conflict these brave men and women face many changes. Traumatized by what they have witnessed they may retreat into a realm of silent emotion. They must learn to cope with a society and government that only faintly remembers their sacrifice. This explains why the brotherhood of combat can be a source of comfort. Until you have walked in the shoes of a soldier you will never know the terror that touches the hearts of those innocently thrown into harm's way.

An extended scenario with those involved in conflict are the lifestyles of the families who either live in violent territories or are the distant families supporting those in combat zones facing the unknowing reality their loved ones may not return home. How would your life change if your family member was sacrificed during conflict?

Other occupations that present the potential of danger include those who serve as police officers, as firefighters, individuals who serve in toxic industries, or those poised as medical caregivers tasked with caring for those inflicted with contagious diseases. I am sure many more dangerous occupational endeavors will come to mind. Often these individuals must cope in silence to protect those involved but the emotional toxicity can be stored within body systems surfacing years after the initial exposure. It is always important to thank the individuals who have assumed roles in dangerous occupations for assuming the role they were specifically designed to engage in.

Earth Challenges: With increasing weather anomalies none can predict with certainty where the next weather extreme will present. With little warning lifetime possessions become only a memory. What once might have been a thriving community could be reduced to remnants of destruction. How would your life change if in an instant you lost your home or family member through disaster? What would be your new order of concern? Can you see how small our world really is when disaster strikes?

Illness/Disease: At any moment any of us could be given a life altering diagnosis. How would you react? Will you succumb to the diagnosis or will you find the determination to overcome your prognosis? A diagnosis need not be a life sentence. Imagine the courageous souls who endure the many months of cancer treatment. If you are the primary bread winner with a life-threatening diagnosis, what concerns will occupy your thinking?

Those enduring lengthy illness, who continue to engage in the activities of daily living are the real masters of life. Steven Hawking comes to mind here. This incredible soul chose to continue to inspire the world with scientific revelations despite his debilitating diagnosis. Those who rise above their restrictions provide inspiration for others who face uncertain futures, perhaps even providing the courage to look to the future and not live in the past.

Injury/Pain: Most will experience pain from an injury or chronic condition at some point in their lives. But until you have experienced chronic pain you may never know how difficult it can be to accomplish the routine activities of daily living. What to you may be a simple routine, to someone who suffers from pain due to injury or disability may be a tremendous accomplishment, if accomplished at all.

I recall a time in my life when I broke my ankle. Just navigating across a parking space to a grocery store was a marathon. My injury was temporary but if anyone suffers from a chronic ailment you can imagine how this impairment could challenge any daily activity. It is easy to take for granted the convenience good health provides. It is a brave individual who refuses to let physical restriction define their living.

Mental Impairment: Any routine life deviation can trigger depression. Even in the smallest doses, depression can turn the most fun-loving person into a sluggish drag. The prolonged effects can further damage daily functioning leading to deeper depression. Caretakers of those experiencing significant mental challenges can also feel the mental exhaustion from the vigilance their care requires. What can we learn about those experiencing depression? What change can we employ to hearing their emotional challenges? What was once considered a taboo topic is now surfacing with greater intensity calling for intervention and coping measures to alleviate the challenge.

Poverty and Financial Hardship: With gloomy financial forecasts, job loss and sketchy economics, no wonder so many have trimmed budgets and still find themselves living on the edge. It would seem few have escaped the world's financial overhaul. However, without feeling the effects of economic restraints, too many might turn a blind eye to the hardship experienced by so many. Cutting corners can mean different things to different financial classes. Some may only experience the inconvenience of dwindling assets while others will face difficult choices of survival. Despite the current world financial budget trimming there are individuals living within the borders of developing countries whose poverty level makes budget constraints by some seem like you have just won the lottery.

What if you had no money to purchase food? Without warning any can find themselves thrown into life circumstances where previous income will no longer cover expenses. Placing your awareness into these conditions may change your perception of what living on the edge can really mean.

Relationship Incompatibility: If you are fortunate, you will never experience partnership separation. It can take years to reset emotional sails. Emotional scars can linger for a lifetime. Unless you have firsthand experience in the relationship corridor, you will never understand the complications this scenario represents. The loss of worth, the inability to love or be loved, the compromise of anticipated lifestyles can lead to a life of mistrust and unfulfilled potential.

Do any of us really know how we will react to any presenting life challenge? Until we have walked in the shoes of another's challenge, we cannot know how we will react what emotion we will experience, how much stress we may endure or what life change we will encounter. Compassion, understanding and a helping hand are the tools of support. It only takes one courageous individual to be a catalyst for change. All life challenge may result in discovering we are something greater than any of us could imagine.

Meditation – Life from a Higher Perspective

Leni Morrison

Begin to get comfortable. Breathe in love and breathe out tension. With each breath find yourself becoming more relaxed.

Focus your awareness on your heart. The topic is learning to understand how you might react if you were faced with any number of challenges. The idea is to allow yourself to reflect on whether you might criticize another for any belief system or action different than your own. Take a moment and review where you may have reacted to the actions of another. Now place yourself in their shoes. What are the surrounding events/lifestyles/beliefs that may contribute to the action?

Become the awakened and embody divine neutrality. You are a Christed Being--one who holds diamond light and walks the path of love. Your task is to release any judgement while inwardly acknowledging with compassion the struggle, the concern, or the misalignment with that individual and clear any attachment.

When you recognize any polarity within, it will be easy for you to return to balance. Practicing neutrality will allow you to become the observer of any challenge without becoming affected by it.

At this moment release any judgment or any harsh criticism. Acknowledge another's unique journey with understanding. If an action is not in alignment with your beliefs, ask your spiritual guardians to help you release any mental connection, *Now*.

Ask for the Holy Spirit to merge with your higher self. Breathe in diamond and golden rays from the central sun into each chakra. Feel the connection to the universal hierarchy. Invite in cosmic Christ consciousness.

Surrender all lower gender aspects known and unknown that are causing unwanted polarity, old programs engaging you in conflict. Collapse all timelines that lead to separation consciousness.

Ask St. Germain to step forward along with the angelic guardians of the amethyst ray to cleanse your fields of perception with violet fire.

Say inwardly three times: I decree the angels of the violet fire walk before me. Clear my timelines and cleanse my auric field. I allow neutrality to unfold in every aspect of my awakened life.

Take another diamond breath in. Release the old earth energies now. Breathe in the new earth realities of unity consciousness.

How to Receive Messages of Light

Jilliana Raymond

Preparing for Magic

I WONDER IF YOU ARE NOTICING PERSONAL CHANGES AS YOU RECEIVE the wisdom messages and energy infusions presented to you now. A few changes I have noticed since beginning an accelerated ascension journey include some of the following:

- Colors are brighter and the air feels fresher.
- Food choices are more selective. If I ingest something my body is not compatible with, there is swift acknowledgement of displeasure from my body.
- I must be highly aware of my projected thoughts. I have noticed when I project a thought, I receive rapid manifestation. This can be a reminder to us that we need to be vigilant about presenting thoughts less positive than our hopeful reflection and try to project more advantageous positivity, especially with all the ruffles in our current world affairs. But if you get flustered and send out a negative vibe, beware that you might experience a swift backlash or experience a significant energy drain.
- I have more energy.

- I notice I'm more sensitive to earth anomalies.
- I am more sensitive to energy.
- I interpret spiritual messages with greater accuracy.
- I have incorporated an ability to allow life interference in without judgement.
- I awaken without conscious awareness of time, day, or date.
- I have a strong desire to detach from drama.
- I experience consistent synchronicities.
- I experience magic within my life. I expect positive outcomes.
- I acknowledge profound insight to evolving life scenarios.
- I find I review my life with gratitude and grace.
- Life seems less complicated. I am able to deal with conflict with assertiveness and understanding.

Humanity is shifting between two characteristics--the spiritual being and the human one. These two characteristics are merging to assist in your becoming one complete individual; spiritually aware, yet able to live in a physical reality without compromising who you are. This represents becoming heart centered. This is the language of God/Source--however you address a higher vibrational sovereign energy. How do you know when you are in alignment with your highest self? When whatever you are doing is in total flow, heart-centered, not needing to force anything, a time where "knowing" is without needing to know but being at peace with whatever needs to happen is exactly right for you. When you reach this point, everything manifests effortlessly.

We are becoming new DNA engineers. I never really thought deeply about this before but if we can grasp the concept that we are the designers of our specific worlds, it makes sense. With this revelation, we are reminded we can rewrite our personal stories. This is huge. If we can heal our present experience, we can heal our past. This is learning to let go of past traumas and restrictions we have imposed upon ourselves not knowing that the experiences we are confronted with can be our best teachers. This is an attempt to shift us out of some event or belief that might be compromising personal lifestyles. For many of us experiencing varied life lessons what we have learned can often take many lifetimes. I am definitely no exception.

Each time we experience a life where trauma has been encountered, more than likely a part of our soul splintered. Our current evolutionary phase is now calling back those splintered parts. How is this being accomplished? Dreams can provide glimpses into past traumas. If you can remember any portion of your dreamscapes, try to recall a particularly disturbing dream reality where you may have awoken in the morning remarking how fretful your night was because of a bothersome dream encounter. More than likely you were releasing a memory from your past, thus calling a fragmented part of your soul back to your present soul incarnation. I should also note here that a particularly disturbing dream will only be presented when the dreamer is ready to release the encounter. Some of our past life experiences have been exceptionally traumatic. Only when your energy frequency has evolved sufficiently will you encounter a past traumatic challenge to be cleared.

Another method you can explore to uncover soul fragments is through meditation where you can experience brief flashbacks of some parallel life. Humanity is leaving the 3D world behind and merging with higher evolved realms. The unfortunate side effect of this merge is chaos as the two dimensions collide.

Spirit sees your *Lights*, just as you see those little flickers of light that manifest in your room at night or when you close your eyes and begin to meditate and you see little diamonds of light. And since the topic of this chapter is *How to Receive Messages of Light*, I thought you might like to see an interpretation of how spirit sees your energy field. The image you are looking at is a "Quantum Activator." If you were standing before the image, you would be able to feel the heart energy emanating from the image. The image may unfortunately not present the vivid color representative of this energy quadrant but just as your auric field is represented by color aspects reflecting your current energy vibration, so too does this Quantum Activator reflect the color dimension of the particular frequency being emitted. Auric photography is a wonderful way to see how your color frequencies are registering your body's reflective pattern. This is not a constant field and fluctuates depending on the exposure to the environmental influences you encounter or the emotional field you are emitting.

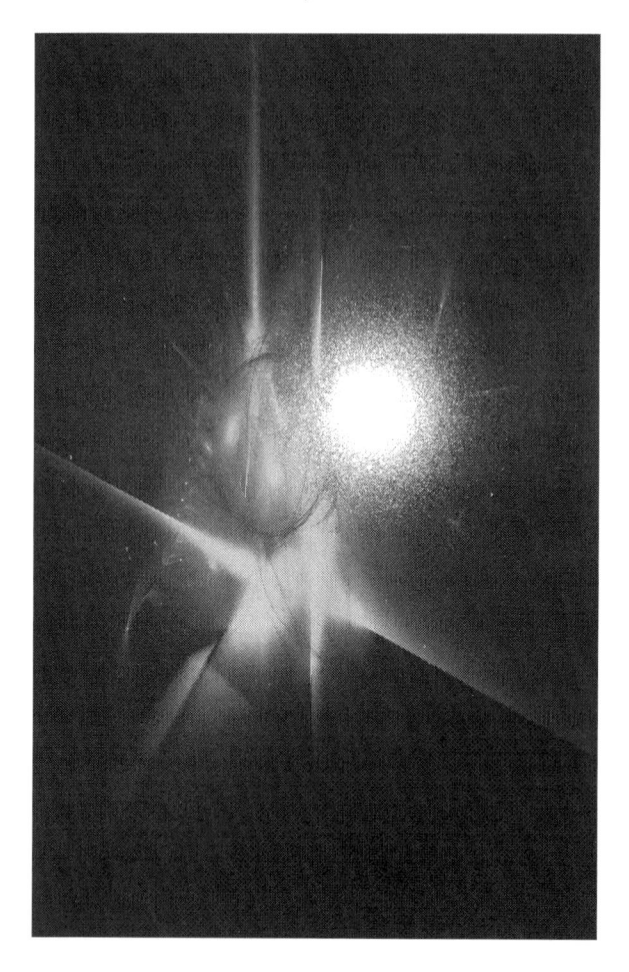

The artwork is from an incredible artist, Andre Ferrella (www.andreferrella.com). Andre is the creator of *"The Spirit Box,"* a 3D immersion with the energy of Jesus. Andre's work has been presented at the Louvre and throughout the world.

Communicating with Spiritual Resources/Source/Creator

I want to talk about communication with Source. I also want to remind you that your God-connection is not external from you but internal from within. You cannot be separate from the field of the Great Is. The need to drive to a

Discovering Your Mastery

sacred site or utilize formal language such as "Dear God" is not necessary. You can initiate contact anywhere, anytime, or in any language. God's true house is in your heart. God is wherever you are, *Always.*

Your conversation might commence with *"Hurry, I need you now!"* or you could start by just saying *"Hi, I want to tell you how much you mean to me."* By the way, spirit loves recognition for the love they send to you. Just as a curious comparison, say your normal prayer without sending any accolades and then say your prayer expressing your gratitude and FEEL the differing energy response.

Another note on prayer is that if you are serious about your request make a declaration to spirit. Your summons might begin something like this; "Provide me with..." This could be far more effective than; "When you get around to it" (etc.) ending with a "please and thank you." Spirit knows what you are going to ask before you ask it. Spirit just wants to be sure you are serious about your request.

What if what you are requesting is not in your best interest or the interest of the individual you are praying for? Spirit sees 360 degrees. On my best day of reflection, I may only see 180.

You were previously presented with the reference to the "still point" of God. I am going to take you on a somewhat simplified exploration on *How You Communicate with God.* When I am counseling individuals who feel stuck because of a certain issue, I ask why not reach out to God? A general response is" I don't want to *bother* God for that." My immediate response is "Why not?" God is not some "Wizard of Oz" person hiding behind a curtain. God is an all-knowing, omnipresent energy. Just for the sake of familiarity, I am going to address this omnipresent energy as "God" with the understanding that no formality is necessary. God is neither *He* nor *She* and there really are no rules when establishing communication with God or *any* of your Light messengers. If you are truly in dire need of God's assistance, do you think you would have to go through an invocation ritual to first establish a link? Absolutely not! You would just start your conversation with I need *Help now*!

Let's look at some guidelines you could use to establish a ritual of communication. God loves to communicate with you. In fact, your spiritual guardians start dancing at the mere thought of engaging with you and are just waiting for your invitation to join in.

When you meditate, pray, or send a thought of gratitude or concern, you are indicating your intention to communicate with God. You are also inviting your spiritual guardians into your life every time you reach out to communicate with God. If you want to address a specific individual or cosmic group, you can solicit engagement with these individuals as well.

I know some of you come from traditional roots so your communication might be a little more formal such as "Dear God." You might also solicit communication with the Archangels in this manner. But your conversation might equally be as simple as: "Yo--God, I have been meaning to ask you about helping me find some extra cash this month." In addition, you might like to light a ritualistic candle or play soft music. If these tools make communication more meaningful for you, by all means employ these techniques.

I do want it clear though that God and your spiritual team hear every prayer, wherever you choose to solicit communication, however you choose to deliver your message. I also want you to know that God does not give more attention to one prayer over another, except in emergencies of course, where manifestation may be a bit more prompt.

Let's talk a little bit about different kinds of prayer. I am making light of prayer intentionally to illustrate that prayer does not need to be a somber recitation of words but should be an open conversation. Can you identify with the pattern of these solicitations?

- There is your urgent prayer; "Come quick, I'm in a real jam."
- There is the "I really need your assistance" prayer, "please respond at your earliest convenience."
- Then there is the "I will put you on my to-do list," repetitive prayer.

It is the intention behind the prayer (the motive) and the amount of emotion generated by the communication that elicits God's attention. Another key element determining the successful outcome of your prayer might include the degree of passion you place behind your request or concern.

Prayer can be a blessing, a thought or concern. You can pray for resolution, healing, forgiveness, answers to your questions or to see if God would intervene on your behalf to bring a desired result. You can ask for money, companionship, employment, health, or peace.

Once I have established the topic(s) for my dialogue I begin to relay my agenda. I usually establish a connection by thanking God, the angels, and my spiritual guardians for being with me during the day's activities. I then like to address local or worldly issues that could benefit from my prayers. Once I have lent my energy to assist in the various current events of the day, I begin to project thoughts and images for future events and requests I would like to have present in my own life. An important annotation here is that I present my request(s) by thanking my spiritual alliance as if my prayer has already been answered. I visualize the benefit of my request as if I am already enjoying it.

Is There a More Optimal Delivery for Prayer?

Have you ever noticed when you really need action that you get a little more intense with your thoughts—like "I need assistance Now!" kind of direction? And have you noticed how quickly you receive assistance? When I need resolution to a specific issue my prayer might be formatted thus: "Provide me with (whatever resolution I am seeking)" rather than "I would appreciate you presenting me with…as soon as possible."

You might try varying solicitations and see which way you receive a higher resolution to your request. I am fairly sure you will get a stronger reaction if you issue an action, rather than a plea for intervention. And--if you have reached your limit, your patience is at an all-time low and your nerves are frazzled, my intonation gets even more intense—something like—"I have had it--I expect your intervention now!" In short, I make a declaration of intent, rather than a plea.

I also add visual cues along with my message. The more detail I provide, the easier fulfillment will be. The spiritual ethers (or as I like to refer to them as the universe) respond very well to visual images. Remember the chapter on *The Quantum Tapestry*--your direct communication awakens a flurry of activity on behalf of your request. When you amplify your declaration with an emotional overlay, this provides the intensity behind the projection… and… repetition amplifies the request.

You might say that prayer is a package deal. If prayer is talking to God, then the quiet reflective period spent after prayer would be the meditative mode that allows you to listen for the answers.

Have You Been Taking God for Granted?

Now, before you start shuddering at the query above, one of my clients was seeking assistance on finding a new job. I inquired if my client made this request of God. Their response was that it was their opinion the request was "too trivial and potentially not worth God's attention." "Too trivial," you say, nothing in God's kingdom is too trivial. God wants to be involved in all aspects of your life, even in trivial matters that involve traffic jams, employment conflicts, what suit to wear and so on. If you have a vested interest in God, it stands to reason that God has a vested interest in you.

Is It Selfish to Ask for Something for Yourself?

Absolutely not! Remember that God has a vested interest in every aspect of your life. God's greatest desire is to see you living a life in health, peace, joy, and abundance. Most of the time it is not God who prevents you from achieving what you desire or need, it is your own misunderstanding of how your thoughts affect your daily life that prevents you from achieving a favorable result. Too often life conditioning causes you to deny success because you either believe you are unworthy of receiving what you desire, or the life contract chosen is a more complicated life experience.

As individuals, we are constantly sabotaging our own well-being through a constant barrage of buts, cant's, improbabilities and maybe tomorrows. These are all remnants of intrusive thinking that contribute to keeping us from achieving a life of our dreams.

Is Your Prayer Enhanced by the Number of Individuals Praying on Your Behalf?

I remember a prayer interpretation that indicates when "two or three are gathered together in God's name, God would grant the request." Certainly, the combined prayers of a few or many individuals focusing their energies on a desired outcome can enhance the result. You might call this the tipping affair or "Bell Curve" enhancement. You see, the universe is not biased on an outcome. Majority rules, so, if the majority sways one way stronger than another that will be the outcome, even if it is an unfavorable one.

Leni Morrison and Jilliana Raymond

Meditation - How to Receive Messages of Light

Leni Morrison

Get comfortable in your meditative space. Begin your meditation by taking in three deep clearing breaths. With every breath become more relaxed, allow distracting thoughts to fade. Call in love, light, and magic.

Activate your crystalline energy body and energize your DNA into the cosmic Christ consciousness to begin to merge with the New Earth consciousness of Gaia.

> Call in your avatar consciousness. State: I command my body of crystalline light to expand.
>
> Connect your heart to the cosmic heart of mother earth.
>
> Connect your spirit to the light of the central sun.

State: My cellular divinity is who I AM. I AM Source consciousness.

State: I now activate my light body. I feel expansion. I am connecting to Source love and light. I am aware that this light is not outside me but within me. Enter into complete stillness. Set an intention to become fully immersed in cosmic light.

Breathe in golden light, diamond golden light particles through your crown chakra.

Inwardly say: I now surrender to my deep faith and feel the light from Source within me. I now fill my third eye with violet light, the violet light infused with diamond golden pearlescent light. Breathe this light into your third eye. Source light is the light in which I see.

I now breathe in the sapphire blue and diamond light into my throat chakra.

I am in alignment with myself and in alignment with Source. I am in alignment with my soul purpose. Source light is the light in which I see.

I am always the embodiment of the true connection to Divine Source. I breathe in pink and diamond light into my heart chakra. Source light is the light in which I see.

I now breathe in pastel yellow and diamond rays into my solar plexus.

My perception of what physical reality is changing. I now know myself as a particle of God, as an image of a Divine spark of God's love. Source light is the Light in which I see.

I now breathe in pastel orange and seafoam green with emerald light into my sacral chakra.

Say inwardly: I am infused with Source Light. Source light is the light in which I see. Bring your awareness to your root chakra.

Breathe in silver golden light.

Feel the connection between heaven and earth strengthen you as you breathe in love and breathe out love.

Inwardly say: Source light is the Light in which I see. It is through my breath, my light that I connect to Source.

Vibrational Resonance

Jilliana Raymond

MOST OF US WILL AGREE WE LIVE WITHIN AN ENERGY ENVIRONMENT. Did you know that energy vibrations and their varying frequencies influence daily encounters? Did you know you can change your vibration and thus the encounters you experience? The more you understand about energy and its magnetic properties, the more control you maintain over your life experience.

It's a Matter of Frequency

The earth's energy frequency is constantly changing. More importantly, the earth's energy frequency is reflective of the conscious energies upon her. Anything that is out of harmony with her energy fields will be balanced. Anything that is out of balance with the intended design of the human template will also be adjusted. This change is helping humanity identify toxic factors that might inhibit the ultimate earth template--a paradise of diversity to be experienced in harmony, peace, and abundance.

The more you understand about energy frequencies, the easier it will be to determine which vibration is more compatible with your lifestyle. Here are some contributing factors.

- Energy exists on band frequencies and each frequency broadcasts with its own unique vibration.
- Everything has its own unique electromagnetic field. The field is represented by either positive or negative charges, depending on the field of energy the frequency is exposed to.
- Higher vibratory fields operate on higher frequencies, thus carry less density.
- Lower fields present with greater density and broadcast on much lower frequency bands.
- The universal spiritual dimension is an energy dimension. There are varying vibratory fields within this spiritual space.
- Generally, the spiritual field represents a higher frequency field. The spiritual dimension broadcasts via light frequencies.
- Thought becomes the energy that generates the light.

While the spiritual dimension is largely holographic, it manifests through energy frequencies interpreted through thought and action. Physical form becomes a transfer station for the holographic energy field. Thus, earth's physical inhabitants become the receivers and projectors of thousands of transmitted thoughts. Think of frequency as tuning to a radio channel, and there are an infinite number of them. Changing frequencies changes the magnetic attraction of the polarized energy field.

Translating frequency into the human element, individuals projecting positive energy expressed through their thoughts and actions carry higher vibrational frequencies and enjoy life with less resistance. Individuals broadcasting on a lower frequency are usually less energized, constantly live within a framework of negative emotions, and quite often experience complicated lives.

Here is another interesting fact when considering compatible frequencies. Like energies attract. If you want to know what frequency you are generating, evaluate those individuals you align with and note how positive or negative their reflection is about their life expression.

If you are an individual with a positive attitude, you most likely attract individuals and opportunities that represent a reflection of your positive frequency. If you are an individual with a negative attitude, you are more likely to attract individuals and events that mirror similar reflections. Understanding your individual projecting energy frequency begins to explain how you attract individuals and events into your presiding vibration that create your life experiences.

If you haven't already guessed it, maintaining a higher frequency is advantageous. Higher frequencies boost immune systems enabling you to resist disease. Those maintaining a higher frequency attract greater opportunity into their lives. In addition, holding a higher frequency allows for better contact with spiritual guardians who may have important information to present to you to assist with your life navigation. Spiritual guardians reside in higher vibratory dimensions. When you express a dense energy system you block communication with those spiritual energies you want to remain in contact with, energies that can lift your spirit and change the unpleasant challenge you are experiencing.

Positive vs Negative

While you navigate through your daily activities you are constantly threading energy pathways. Wherever your travels take you, you are absorbing and transmitting the various energy frequencies that you encounter. You either acquire a positive charge, reflective of the positive environment of the individuals you encounter or a negative one, specifically if you have entered an area that carries a lower and often volatile frequency. Perhaps your travels have exposed you to individuals who have unknowingly absorbed the toxic elements of their exposure. If all your encounters represent positive influences, then your physical experience will remain positive, thus acting as a magnet, attracting opportunity and synchronistic encounters. This reflection assists to provide you with an understanding that you attract those energies that are a vibrational match to every positive energy exchange. If, on the other hand, you are surrounded in an environment that can potentially reflect a negative atmosphere or the individuals you may encounter present a contentious characteristic, these encounters could contribute to a toxic lifestyle as you will likely absorb the energy residue of your uncomplimentary exposure.

If you perpetuate in life patterns that are unhealthy to your well-being, these unpleasant patterns and their toxic effects will become amplified in your experience. This will affect relationships, jobs, health, where you reside, how rich your life experience can be and how you feel. When you can identify portions of your living experience that require adjustment, you only need to remove yourself from the compromising energy.

Elevating your energy frequency can be as simple as changing your thoughts, incorporating a practice of daily meditation, expressing gratitude, immersing yourself in love or showing compassion. Tuning to a higher energy frequency will enhance your life experience. Staying at a lower frequency will complicate it. It is that simple.

Thoughts Are Energy

All thought creates the future activities in your life. Keep in mind that the intention behind the desired result can work for or against you. If an intense emotion is fueled by a desire to harm, retaliate or create a negative result, you will likely become the recipient of an undesirable backlash. If a generated emotion is fueled with positive intention, you can anticipate a positive outcome. When fear creeps in and attempts to disrupt the faith of any positive projection, it can negate all the positive reflection invested in a desired result.

Incidentally, in case you believe that scheming to deceive or projecting intention to cause harm to another is undetectable, thoughts directed at causing mayhem carry significant consequences. What you do in life matters. How you live your physical life determines how you will experience your life in spirit. You alone become accountable for your actions. There is no review board upon this life exit. There is, however, a personal soul review of your life and an internal desire to rectify less than optimal interactions. It's that "do-over" card that makes you want to erase any compromising frequency.

Money Is Energy

What value do you attach to money? What if you look at money as the energy exchange used to acquire the staples of daily living? How you regard money indicates how you either limit or attract abundance into your life. Consider the following concepts:

- ➤ If you believe you will never have enough you will always have limiting resources.
- ➤ If you regard those who have greater wealth than your own as undeserving, you have closed a door of opportunity to bring that same gain into your life.
- ➤ When the only goal in financial gain is at the expense of others, the business you represent will not generate the required funds to provide long term abundance. The message is that when you compromise another's worth, you project an energy of lack that eventually halts your own flow of abundance.
- ➤ You must feel abundantly wealthy from within before you can experience it externally.

What you focus on most is what you receive. If you only see limitation, so will your bank account. However, if you see your account growing, remaining in gratitude for the ability to cover your expenses, your account will grow. You can visualize a balance that represents your positive reflection before funds become available.

Energy Vampires

Because you are an energy being, emotional attitudes can be superimposed upon you without your conscious awareness. When your energy wattage burns brightly but you are surrounded by individuals who may experience an amp shortage; you may unwittingly be giving your light (energy) to those with lower amperage. Energy leakage can be stimulated by strong emotions of grief, trauma, illness, or social disruption.

If your energy body is not properly insulated, you can experience an energy drain. You can increase your light frequency by connecting to Source (solar energy) and request an energy infusion to eliminate any lower vibrational energy that may have inadvertently attached to your energy frequency. This connectivity should instantly renew your optimistic positive flow. You can also practice energy grounding techniques.

Grounding Technique

You can easily restore your energy by anchoring cosmic light energy into your energy system to assist in soothing fractured nerves, reducing stress and amplifying your energy. Visualization serves as the technique to promote this regenerative tool instantly. See yourself melting into a tree. The trunk becomes your torso, your lower limbs become the roots and your upper limbs become the branches. Send your upper limbs into the heavens, extend your lower limbs deep into the core of the earth. You are now connecting to the energy of the heavens above and the creative, restorative energy of the earth beneath your feet. Anything not in sync with your energy frequency or not presenting a *Love* vibration then bounces off.

You encounter power struggles when you are exposed to individuals whose own energy is weak, thus necessitating an energy infusion from a higher vibrational source. Regardless of your ability to "*SEE*" energy fields, your subconscious field is *ALWAYS* aware of surrounding energy frequencies. So, when one's energy is low, the subconscious seeks a higher energy to restore the weaker one.

Most of us are unaware of our energy liability until others begin to remark on how uncomfortable it has become to be in our presence. It is always easy to determine if we have become the source of an energy picnic, as your energy body begins to recognize the negative drain as sudden fatigue, onset of nausea, headache, uncharacteristic irritation, or emotional lability. Empathic individuals are exceptionally susceptible to unknowingly absorb lower frequency energy fields, especially if they have not insulated their energy fields sufficiently before stepping out into the exterior world of frequency.

If you are involved in a negative confrontation, it is always best to first remove yourself from the source if possible. Simply recognizing the toxic exchange as a power drain can provide you with the wisdom to handle the situation. Remember you can use a variety of light tools to defray the confrontation if walking away is not possible. You can surround the individual in light; put them in a box of mirrors, call in spiritual assistance (I recommend Archangel Michael for confrontation issues), or if you feel your energy field has been assaulted you can conduct a brief conflict resolution session to speak directly to the individual's higher self to seek resolution.

Most earth inhabitants have experienced emotional fatigue. A good representation of emotional fragmentation could be expressed through any familiar life encounter such as natural disaster, a worldwide lock down due to Covid fatigue or the fragmented energy drain any political fatigue has presented. Of late, earth has also been dealing with astrologic pulses from varying planetary alignments. When planets are retrograde (planetary alignments moving in reverse) it can cause edginess amongst planetary inhabitants. When the planets are progressing forward and the planetary configurations are in alignment with your birth cycles, you are most likely able to navigate activities with less resistance. In addition to the planetary rotations within our cosmic network, the earth and her inhabitants have experienced extremely powerful magnetic infusions through a multitude of solar flares, rare planetary alignments and an increase in lunar and solar eclipse activity. These are extremely elementary explanations by the way but may help you understand how all universal elements play into daily lives.

Alternative Therapeutic Energy

Alternative energy therapies will become more prominent in maintaining healthy living in earth inhabitant futures. An increasing number of complimentary therapies to traditional medical intervention will become more main stream. The focus will be on prevention. Many of you may already be practitioners in alternative modalities. Some newer modalities include sound and light therapies. There are multiple emerging therapies that are proving to be useful techniques in smashing calcifications within internal organs utilizing sound, soothing arthritic joints using light frequencies or utilizing specialized laser techniques during surgical procedures for example. In addition, cryotherapy is emerging in alternative protocols and new experimentation with cellular reconstruction using stem cell therapies, DNA harvesting (CRISPR) and many more advanced technologies on the healing horizon.

Many individuals practice some form of Reiki. This is a gentle energy infusion designed to reduce stress and provide a conduit for the body to begin to heal. Other energy modalities include massage, reflexology, craniosacral therapy, acupressure, or acupuncture. To some degree these energy therapies work with body meridians unlocking congested energy circuitry to allow the body to realign and establish internal communication once again.

Earth Energy

The earth's energy is changing. She is repositioning in the solar system as she crosses her galactic center, the Milky Way. While she is realigning in the cosmos, her magnetic frequency is changing as the earth is introduced to new magnetic influences. With the earth's new magnetic position, so too are your energy frequencies changing. As the earth moves into a higher vibrational dimension the physical inhabitants upon her are experiencing changes from an old 3D template to the progressive crystalline template that can carry higher frequency fields.

Everything upon earth is vibrating at different frequencies--from the products you purchase, to the food you consume, to the people you encounter, or the places you visit. Every country, individual city, or neighborhood of residence carries its own frequency. Each frequency is generated by the collective inhabitants of that region. Most earth inhabitants may not be aware that the land and environment in which they reside carry their own energy frequency.

If you are finding it difficult to adjust to a new location it more than likely means that your energy is not compatible with the energy frequency of that region. If your relocation finds you endlessly exploring your new environment, meeting new individuals, and feeling good about your move, then this is validation your energy is a complete match with your new residence. There is an astrologic study called cartography that can identify regions that match specific vibrations to locations. This is generally correlated through your personal astrologic chart. It is said your life is mapped out in the stars. This analysis can usually provide you with multiple choices to provide you with a choice of preferred residence.

Just for Fun

Here are some energy exercises you can do to familiarize yourself with energy, as well as accelerate your intuitive faculties.

Exercise 1: Working with plants

Most individuals have a plant in their residence. Hopefully, it is a healthy plant. Start by placing the palm of your dominant hand approximately 10 inches above the plant. Slowly move your hand closer to the leaves until you feel the surrounding energy field. This could feel like a slight prickliness on your palm, warmth or a feeling that could be described as encountering a denser field. If you are having difficulty establishing a connection with your plant, ask verbally (aloud) for your plant to raise its vibration so you can feel its energy field. Repeat the above sequence until you are successful at experiencing the energy field.

You can communicate with your plant. Ask where your plant wants to be, in what room, or how much light it wants to receive. If you have several plants, ask which plant would like to be next to another. You are receiving intuitive responses through a thought that spontaneously presents in your mind, not necessarily verbally from the plant. The plant will respond by growing healthier, producing more flowers, even telling you when it needs to be watered. It does take a little practice. When arranging multiple plants with each other ponder how you feel when the correct configuration is acquired. You will remark to yourself--that's it--that feels right. This exercise acknowledges how connected you really are to your surrounding environment.

Exercise 2: A memory journey

This is a memory journey that eventually you will be able to apply to everywhere you go. As you are reading through the exercise, try to recall details that will have telling messages for you.

You are looking for a new residence. You have searched online and now it's time to drive by your location. Pay attention to your surrounding area. You don't want to live next to a landfill, an electrical grid that might interfere with your frequency, a flood zone, a dry zone (unless you enjoy the desert), a volcanic zone, or what I'm going to categorize as a "dead zone" (living in close proximity to a cemetery or any battle zone that could be energy compromising). This is of course unless you wish to experience the lingering energy of the inhabitants within burial zones. You also want to reside next to pleasant neighbors surrounded by a pleasing environment. But how are you going to accomplish this? You're going to sense the energy in the area. Ask questions to see how you internally respond to those questions. How well-kept is the neighborhood? Are there neighbors outdoors? Do they wave as you pass by or do they look suspiciously at you? If you sense a pit in your stomach (a little flip flop of anxiety) or if what you were hoping to see does not meet all your expectations, this is not a compatible energy for your specific field. Conversely, if you get excited about the location, the residence, and you feel an exuberant excitement about the potential property, your subconscious energy is acknowledging your enthusiasm and potential positive compatibility.

You can apply this energy formula to assessing every environmental area you enter. You will notice across your journey where the land is sad, the energy is low, or even if that car you've been looking at is your car. Your energy journey will present you with information about a store that has some desirable surprise inside and indicate which storefront to avoid. Your energy exploration will even let you know which seat you will sit in when you attend any function.

Ghostly Affair

I thought this might be a fun exploration. I have been known to do a bit of ghost hunting or should I say battlefield clearing. Anyway, if you are buying an older residence it may come with a previous owner. How will you tell? Do you get the willies when you walk inside? Does hair stand up on your arms? Do you feel like your hair is being played with? I live in an historic town where many local restaurants and homes have auxiliary residents. Most of the residual inhabitants are friendly but if you reside near an area that experienced violent conflict, it is best to look elsewhere for your perfect residence.

I am used to living with a ghost and have even felt protected by one when I lived on a battlefield. But this may not be acceptable for you. For our European and international readers, there is most likely an abundance of lingering souls amongst the lands. Foreign landmarks carry extensive ancestral energies. If you are interested in moving into a new housing development, you may want to research the prior land use before signing a contract.

Energy Reflections

All souls enter the earth's environment with high-vibrational core energy. None start out intending to be the latest terrorist or narcissistic dictator du jour. Certainly, no one desires to become the latest offender or victim. None need endure life threatening disease. You should now understand that all are influenced by whatever energy exposure defines their life experience. All are shaped by those individuals that filter in and through their lives. All are influenced by family relationships, cultural traditions, those we define as teachers, leaders, lovers, and friends. All contribute to your energy engagements. What you learn and inherit from family imprints usually sets the foundation for your creative life experience.

If you are taught to love and grow within a supportive and benevolent environment, you will hopefully maintain that positive influence. If, however, your life observation is one of turmoil, restriction, and condemnation it becomes more difficult to separate from the foundation you have become accustomed to during your formative years. Understanding the energy components of the individuals, cultures and environments that define your surrounding communities helps you understand the source of your presenting imbalance.

If you continue to absorb lower modulating energy frequencies without eliminating their toxic effects, you will continue to lower your core frequency. How you expose your energy systems to your entire living world determines how sustainable your energy body becomes. Most importantly, you can change any aspect of an unbalanced environment once you recognize the components contributing to a positive or negative charge.

Meditation – Vibrational Resonance

Leni Morrison

Begin to relax. Start by taking in three deep breaths through your nose and expelling the air through your mouth. With each breath you will relax deeper, allowing any external noise to fade away.

Breathe in love and breathe out all that does not represent love. Call in all that you are, all that you ever were and all that you will ever be into this moment. Fill every fiber of your being with golden light. Hold this golden light in your energy system. Give thanks for the highest, purest energies to fill and surround you now. Breathe out gold.

Set your intention that just for now you are going to release all lower energy you may have absorbed because of exposure to any lower frequency. Seize this opportunity to delete parts of you that no longer represent your sovereignty. Release any identity that represents that of a victim. As best you can release any energy of wounding. Release any broken part of you and release anything that is not dressed in pure love now.

Release any uncomplimentary energy that is draining your energy life force. Purify the energy between you. Breathe in golden light into the field and begin to feel your vibration rise.

Release anything that is not heart aligned. Let it dissolve. Fill your renewed energy sphere with love, forgiveness and only memories that uplift your spirits. Breathe in golden light. Hold the golden light. Give thanks for the golden light. Breathe out golden light.

This is the year of big revelations. It may be hard to process some of your friends and family may choose a different path than yours. Awaken to your power. Say 'Yes' to what feel is right for you from this moment forward.

Say 'Yes' to experiencing your original source light—light that streams from your heart to hearts of humanity that act as magnetic fields. This is the unity consciousness field. Once again breathe in golden light. Hold the golden light. Give thanks for the golden light. Breathe out gold.

Know you are not alone. Your light will shine to attract the appropriate individuals to you. Your light family sparkles like diamonds in the human energy field. Nothing can take your light. It will never leave.

You are now rising above false programming, distractions, energy vampires, choosing to love and not fear, keeping positive based energy. Say 'Yes' to the infinity spark that you carry within your heart. This is your time to be authentic. Start to see everything in your life experience that gives you opportunistic choices.

Who's in Your Soul Family?

Jilliana Raymond

THIS IS THE CHAPTER WHERE WE BEGIN TO EXPLORE WHO IS IN YOUR soul family and how you will recognize these individuals. In addition, we are also going to explore how you determine which soul contracts you choose, why you choose them and what implications are received based on your choices.

By now, I hope you are comfortable knowing your current physical journey is just another exploration into your soul's composition while your spirit is housed in a physical form. In your prior journeys you may have visited several cosmic civilizations, helped in the evolutionary process of humanity over millennia and explored countless life lessons, all designed to add another component to your soul's desire to acquire the wisdom and experience each incarnation provides.

Guides and Guardians

I am hopeful you are assured you have never been alone during your physical journey. In fact, you have always had an army of souls and a spiritual ensemble assisting you throughout your endeavors. One incredibly special guardian has been with you throughout your lifetimes. This soul has direct wisdom to help steer you to make the most appropriate choices for your experience. This individual has never been part of your soul family. Now that leads me to an interesting discussion. It has taken lifetimes for your guardian to train to become your life guide. This soul knows you intimately, has experienced the life you are living, or the one you are planning to experience. With direct knowledge of the complications and paths you might choose, this individual can be that little whisper in your ear that provides you with the knowledge to accomplish the lesson you have chosen or try to prevent you from taking that path where the bridge is out.

I should note that this guardian will adamantly inform you that you are the individual who must live your life. There will be guidance to help you navigate through your varying scenarios, but your guide cannot and will not interfere with the choices you make during your physical journey--even if it means you may engage in a less than optimal experience. I might remind you here, there is NEVER any judgement for any choice you make, even if it leads you down a path that may not be advantageous. The guidance from your guide may remind you there might have been a better way to accomplish the lesson you were attempting to master but these souls know there are always multiple pathways to accomplish many lessons.

Soul Clusters

Members of your soul family are individuals you have spent lifetimes with. Every individual is unique with varying personalities compatible with your frequency. These are individuals you recognize with ease. You can conduct a spontaneous conversation with any of these souls picking up wherever you left off—even if you have not seen these individuals for millennia. Each time you reunite there is a subtle familiarity and instant connectivity. Perhaps you encounter a stranger on your path that you don't initially recognize. You might remark however, "Don't I know you from somewhere?"

You may spend moments, days, months, years, or a lifetime with these individuals in physical fellowship. The individual roles may vary but there will be a compatible thread in your present life philosophy so there is little gap between your initial conversation or a review of personal points of interest. Roles during physical lifetimes also vary. I will spend a little time discussing this aspect of your soul cluster further on.

Members of your soul family may be physical family member(s), a romantic partner, best friend(s), or a collection of individuals you interact with on a regular or infrequent basis. Individuals may appear at an appropriate moment to present some alliance you have chosen to pursue. The timing of this encounter could have been pre-programmed long before you entered onto the earth plane to explore your physical journey. (And yes...you pre-planned your journey before you incarnated). You may be the individual who presents to provide some support for your soul family member. Again, the timing of these encounters is usually specifically aligned. You do not need to know the details of a coming encounter as the universe and your subconscious programming are always impeccably aligned and aware of every encounter.

While it is uncertain how many souls are represented in your soul cluster, it is presumed clusters may consist of approximately one hundred souls. To help you visualize a soul cluster, picture a tree glistening with the lights of the souls this tree contains. Picture also there is a forest of trees, all glistening with the lights of their respective soul clusters. This can appear like a thousand star lights or a tree filled with fire flies. Now you can see how very bright the universe really is. Your universe is a Light wonderland represented by the millions of souls that comprise your universal collective.

Popular thought may lead you to believe all members of your physical family represent members of your soul cluster. This is generally not an accurate assessment. Before your incarnation you made an agreement with the individuals who would be your biologic parents in this life. You chose this association to help you accomplish your life task.

Are Mom and Dad Part of My Soul Family?

Your biologic parents may not be members of your soul cluster but assist in fulfilling your soul agreement. We all know not all parents take parenting roles seriously and may in fact lead to complicating lives. Remember your biologic parents represent the individuals you chose to provide you either with the vehicle for your earth entry so you could be present during the galactic shift or provide you with the foundation to smoothly transition into an established life profession.

Are My Siblings Part of My Soul Family?

While your siblings are members of your physical family, they may not be part of your soul family and may have their own contract with your biologic parents. This may explain often contentious differing opinions amongst family siblings. And remember, your siblings have joined your family unit for the same reasons you have entered your family grouping.

The differing voices amongst your family dynamics may provide an important catalyst for you to engage in a specific life journey. And just to confuse family interactions a little further, your roles may intertwine between your biologic family members from lifetime to lifetime and still not represent those individuals who reside within your immediate soul family.

Recognizing Soul Family Members

Now that the ground rules of family membership have been identified, how do you recognize family individuals who may be members of your soul family? These individuals might be recognized by the closeness of your association with one or more members of your physical family. You might wish to explore deep reflection on the connectivity you share with family members. Despite the loving connection you may share with all family members, which of those individuals represent the eternal connection that is part of your soul family? Are you closer to one parent over the other? Are you close to a specific grandparent? Is there one sibling you feel a special connection to? You can extend this assessment to cousins, aunts, uncles, and extended family members. The diversity of splitting your soul family into different pods is by universal design.

For those able to receive direct communication with your guardians and guides you can ask them directly if one member or another is part of your soul cluster. This exercise may also serve to enhance your ability to receive communication with your spiritual entourage and enhance your energy sensitivity.

I have addressed how you might recognize soul members within your family composition but let's explore how you will recognize those individuals who represent soul cluster inclusion throughout your extended relationship encounters. You may be in committed relationship. Relationships may or may not be shared with a member from your soul cluster. Often agreements are made with individuals from other soul clusters to become those committed members you share your intimate engagements with. Each encounter represents an agreement you pre-determined to be essential for your soul's evolution. This would explain some encounters that do not satisfy lasting physical companionship. However, if you share a committed relationship with a soul partner, this individual is most probably a member of your personal soul cluster.

Acquaintances are generally not members of your immediate soul family. These individuals provide you with timely information, interaction, or activity but rarely represent individuals who participate as soul cluster members. Friends, on the other hand, can be members within your specific pod. Again, you will recognize these individuals by the instant familiarity. However brief your interaction with those you engage in activity with, the support provided during your interaction can be uplifting.

Soul Cluster Members in Spirit

Not all your soul family is in physical residence at the same time as your current incarnation. Many remain behind to provide additional steerage along your journey. Some alliances may be so strong that there is a permanent attachment to you while you reside in your physical space. In fact, several close relationships between friends and soul companions reside within their spiritual residence while you are in your physical residence.

What is the Purpose of Your Soul Cluster?

Members of your soul family are all compatible in vibration regardless of the lessons each individual chooses to fulfill. Each member has achieved lifetimes of experience from the varying incarnations each has explored. Many will have interstellar interactions with other civilizations. All lessons will be shared with the individuals in each soul cluster. As the collective vibration of your cluster accelerates in frequency, more experiences emerge to explore. Generally, all members will be researchers of a specific area. For instance, should your cluster be individuals researching fields in medicine, most of your membership will include those members embarking on the same resource of study. Should your cluster be in training to be guardians or guides of physical life forms, your cluster will reflect this area of expertise. Should your cluster consist of explorers/adventurers, membership will include those individuals who desire to excel in these fields. These explorers are your Magellans, Columbus, or John Glenns and so on. Should your cluster focus be those individuals practicing healing arts, then many of your soul family will represent healing pathways. Is your focus in the arts? Then your cluster consists of Mozarts, Bethovens, Picassos, Michaelangelos, Jane Austens, Mark Twains and so on. If your cluster purpose is scientific, then your members may include Einstein, Marie Curie, Isaac Newton, or perhaps Stephen Hawking. Perhaps you are a universal Ambassador; members here will be those individuals who become planetary teachers.

Importance of Soul Family Learning

Not all soul cluster members are off world in one incarnation. Cluster members rotate in and out of spiritual residence depending on the timing, frequency and group lessons being explored. If you belong to a particularly advanced soul family, then learning experiences may be more complex. The soul is always seeking to expand in knowledge and awareness.

For example: Say your cluster's focus is scientific or medical and you want to experience as many medical or scientific scenarios as possible, you might divide the learning experiences between members of your soul family. Every time one soul member accomplishes/overcomes the challenge of that physical exploration, the entire cluster becomes the benefactor by absorbing the results of that learning experience without individually having to endure the challenges the incarnating individual experienced.

Soul lessons may include overcoming addiction, abandonment, anger, poverty, even illness. If your soul cluster's purpose is becoming a life guide, it will require lifetimes of physical experience to be able to provide steerage for a multitude of challenges the soul the spirit guide has been given charge over may encounter. You must be prepared and must decide which challenges you will engage in to be able to provide the best steerage. It would be inconceivable to take on the life challenges of all the required components necessary to be well versed in all of the surrounding complicating scenarios. This is why it becomes necessary to reincarnate to explore the varying dimensions of multiple life scenarios.

If you are the individual who has overcome a significant challenge during this physical life, know that your achievement is benefiting your entire soul cluster. This is the calling of a Master. The harder the soul challenge, the higher the spiritual master. Soul clusters may intertwine once mastery has been achieved. Say you have mastered the life encounters you desired to explore, and you now wish to progress onto further exploration in a different cluster. You will graduate from your current cluster and move onward into your new area of exploration. So, you see, you really are extraordinary. Nothing you do is unimportant.

I hope this gives you a broad overview of the complexities and inclusions of your soul family providing you with a new awareness of the members who comprise this select grouping.

Leni Morrison and Jilliana Raymond

Meditation - Who's in Your Soul Family?

Leni Morrison

Get comfortable and begin to relax. It's okay to drift in and out. There are no rules as healing energy goes where it needs to.

Breathe in golden light three times. Call in your soul family now, those known to you and those unknown to you. Begin to sense and feel who represent members of your soul family with this experience.

Become immersed in your soul body now. Receive the inner healing codes from your soul family and connect to the purest universal energy. Release all old templates as you awaken to your potential, your spiritual essence. Allow your beauty and all that you are to be revealed. Feel the angelic part of you being caressed by the light above.

If you feel any restrictive energies, invoke clearing energies from the violet fire and emerald codes to release any energy that does not reflect your total essence.

Breathe in golden light. Remember you hold the light within you with each breath. You are the purity of light and a spark of divine creativity. Ask your higher self and soul family to assist you now with this healing journey.

The highest, purist and most divine energies are now healing your body and immune system. Say inwardly: Upgrade my source connection to my soul family. Repeat this three times.

Fill your body with strength and vitality and see your energy fields protected. No energy can infiltrate your light or lower your energy field that can deplete your health without your soul permission. You are fully embodied in this reality to transmute all lower energy fields now. Allow your inner force of golden light to build within you while you hold the sacred sound vibration of the universe within your body. These words are light encoded for your

Discovering Your Mastery

own healing. As your light grows from within it expands out into the world. You are birthing a new human, a more empowered human.

The new higher frequencies that you now embody are needed on the planet at this time. You are being called to be a golden emissary of light. Your vibration will carry the earth to a new level. Call in your soul family to assist you through this ascension process. The power of your source connection releases you from anything that is no longer working for you.

Breathe in love, breathe in purity and let this energy heal you now. Shed any residual energy from old templates or previous boundaries and realign with pure love. With this clearing your connection to Source Light energy will increase releasing any further pain or trauma. You are now in perfect alignment with the highest energies on Mother Earth.

Breathe in silver blue diamond light. Merge with Gaia's freedom pathways of crystalline light. Allow Gaia's ascension energy to move up through your feet and legs. You are anchoring the highest consciousness of you into the earth grid that will benefit your entire soul family.

With love and deep gratitude from your soul family, this healing is complete.

Connecting with Your Inner Child

Jilliana Raymond

For ages we have been taught that everything that happens is predetermined. While there is a certain element of truth to this statement, it negates how powerful your own creative intervention can be. Humanity is becoming aware of inner mechanisms that signal not only how you create your living environment, but how you can change your living environment. Becoming aware of the inner language of your inner consciousness is the key. When you learn how to interpret your inner wisdom, you harness the ability to change your living environment.

Meditation will assist in determining what emotional element is creating imbalance and ultimately the events in your life. Communicating with your inner consciousness will determine how you can redirect the subconscious to create optimal benefits that can unfold within your life. Too often it is presumed the conscious mind is the steerage mechanism propelled by thought. But just like computer programs that run unseen performing multiple tasks to accomplish a variety of directions, the subconscious mind is generating the actions that create how you experience your life. Getting in touch with this consciousness is paramount. By listening to your inner wisdom, you will be able to interpret warning signals, that when heeded, will allow you to navigate more efficiently through life challenges.

The meditation that follows will introduce you to what may be referred to as your inner child. This child has also been referred to as your joy guide. If you are not experiencing joy in your life, this is the first indication that something is not in balance with your life. Communication with your inner child will help you determine if there is any life disturbance that needs to be balanced and when this imbalance was recorded in your subconscious. Once the origin of imbalance is identified you will be able to correct it.

Before you begin the meditation, here are some thoughts to keep in mind. As always, meditation begins by finding a quiet, comfortable place where you can focus on the intention of the meditation. You can play soft music in the background if this helps your Zen. Meditation always begins with three deep clearing breaths to allow you to relax and access your inner wisdom. Breathe deeply through your nose and blow the breath out through your mouth releasing tension or stress that may have been building internally. Here is a suggestion for you to receive a deeper connection with your inner child. Either have an individual read the meditation to you or pre-record the meditation to listen to at your leisure. You might also consider sharing the meditation with a group of friends. One individual can read aloud the meditation and the group can then share their experiences to further validate your communication.

Inner Child Meditation

Jilliana Raymond

With each breath find yourself relaxing deeper, releasing external sound or inner noise. Call in your guardians and inform your inner child you wish to establish communication. As your inner child begins to make their presence known to you, focus your attention on the age of the child. This age will change as you mature and release burdensome memories from past trauma.

Notice the expression of your inner child.

> ➢ Is your child playful, sad, or feeling alone?
> ➢ Is your child angry or fearful?

Discovering Your Mastery

- See if your child brings up any memory of discomfort or concern.
- Is there anyone else present in the memory?
- See how many details you can recall. Where are you? Are you outdoors? Are you in a room? Who is in the room with you?
- Do you recall a specific location, perhaps a different state or country?
- Are you listening to a conversation?
- Can you tell what is being said?
- Are you observing an unsettling event? Know that you are observing a memory through your child's eyes.

Take several moments now to conduct discussion with your inner child. After you have identified a volley of inquiries with your inner child you can now reassure your inner child that you are now an adult, and the events of your past will not be present in the future. Explain to your inner child that you are now able to protect your child and that through your experiences and perception as an adult you can prevent further harm. Draw your inner child close to you and hold your child lovingly in your arms. Take hold of this child's hand and reassure them you will guide them wisely through the rest of your life journey providing whatever support necessary.

Once you have made a personal connection, notice if your child's emotion has changed? Have you resolved any fear that may have been present? Has your child's age changed? Is your child older, perhaps now a young adult? Know that if you can address the emotional energy of your inner child, you will forever change the events in your life. Continue to reassure your inner child that you will never allow your child to be alone, to be afraid, to be ignored or misunderstood.

Now ask if there are further messages your inner child would like to tell you? You may ask your inner child any question. Be ready to listen for their response. Their response will be the first impression you receive. Take a moment now to continue your conversation with your inner child.

Your inner child is also considered your joy guide. Ask your inner child what you can do for them that will spark joy? Does your child require something gratifying such as ice cream cone, a walk in the park, a nature hike, or does your child desire a big hug? Provide this for your child noting you are the adult and will be able to determine what is in your child's highest good. Honor their request and follow through by providing them with their request as best as you can. Your inner child holds the keys to your life journey and although their age may come from the presentation of a child, their age does not represent their wisdom.

You can acquire guidance from your inner child whenever you like. This is the inner voice that is constantly chatting at you. At times, the voice will be defiant, critical, and scared. It will be your task to acknowledge this voice, not giving in to the whim but providing guidance and reassurance. Let your inner child know that you are aware of their feelings. If it is in your highest good you will implement necessary changes to improve any compromising scenario. Once you have established a solid bond with your inner child you will be able to provide and receive valuable information regarding the various choices you make during your life.

After you have completed your dialogue and have thanked your inner child for revealing themselves, take a deep breath in through your nose, blowing out any resistance through your mouth. Open your eyes, and as you do you begin to feel lighter, more confident, knowing your new revelations will now provide you solid guidance.

Meditation - Connecting with Your Inner Child

Leni Morrison

Begin clearing by taking three deep breaths in through your nose and expelling your breath through your mouth. With each breath you will find you are going deeper into a reflective space.

Call down a radiant ascension column of diamond and golden light.

Call in all that you are, ever were and ever will be into your space.

Invite in all the celestial guides and galactic star beings that are in a vibrational match to your soul.

Prepare to connect with twenty-four divine beings of illumined light. These include twelve divine masculine energies and twelve divine feminine energies in perfect alignment and balance with your vibration. These energies will help you anchor divine love and unity through sacred consciousness.

Breathe through all the dimensions from the third dimension to the twelfth dimension now. Through your breath, gently breathe your way up through the realms, layers, and levels of consciousness. Upon reaching the twelfth dimension you see a sparkling emerald and pink tourmaline temple. Acknowledge your divine feminine energy revealing itself to you on your left side. Now begin to sense your divine masculine energy revealing its light to you on your right side. Start to get a sense of what your divine spirit looks like. Play with the images and messages that come to you through your extended light streaming to you through your third eye.

Go deep now and embrace the divine feminine love from your higher self. Visualize the pink lotus flower growing in your heart and expanding out in spirals and waves of illumined love. Experience the flow of divine feminine energy wrapped in the rose gold flames of self-love. Feel the energies of intuition, vulnerability, compassion, gentleness, beauty, flexibility, and grace moving into every cell of your being now. Feel the divine feminine courage and unconditional love.

Now embrace your divine masculine spirit. Receive the gifts of the diamond and sapphire sword of light. Place this gift now in your sacred high heart. Call in the gifts of trust, reliability, respect, wisdom, stillness, protection, and empowerment.

Inwardly say: I feel safe. I feel the wise counsel of my heart. I can rely on my divine masculine spirit. I see my divine masculine and my divine feminine merging into one sacred union that amplifies each diamond infused heart petal within my illumined heart. I sense the divine Light codes reconnecting and amplifying in every cell of my being.

I am all that I am.
I am an avatar in this moment.
I now merge with my oneness in all directions of time and space.
I promise to love and honor the voice of my inner child, the Golden Phoenix Child within my sacred center.

I honor the voice within me that is worthy of the deepest love and self-respect, the voice of sovereignty, and the voice of innocence that leads me to the golden pathway of Source Light within me.

I ask this Phoenix Child to sit before me now. I hug this child and look into the eyes of this child now. I speak to and listen closely to my inner child. I tell this consciousness I love you; I hear you, and I appreciate you.

Ask your inner child to forgive you for not nurturing him/her when you were called. Inwardly say: Forgive me for not loving you. Forgive me for not giving you attention. Forgive me for getting angry with you. Forgive me for being childish. Allow me to love you again. I am here for you now and eternally.

Now feel original Source Light all around you and within you shining brighter than ever before. You are now ready to receive the resurrection codes of your I Am presence.

Experience yourself as the cosmic heart of all creation. You are one with all life. Say inwardly: I am one with all life. I now flow with unity consciousness. I am love. I am worthy of the great love. Provide this for me now. Thank those Light Beings who responded to your request. Thank your higher self. Thank the angels. Begin to descend from the higher realms but retain the higher vibration. Anchor this vibration as you return to your earth home, into the crystal heart of Gaia.

As you begin to integrate your energy back into the earth dimension, take a deep breath, open your eyes. Feel renewed, energized, feel the crystalline energy as it flows through you.

And so it is.

Your Conscious Universe

Jilliana Raymond

IT IS TIME TO INTRODUCE YOU TO THE CONSCIOUS WORLD IN WHICH YOU reside. I am certain this information will cause you to pause and reflect upon the nuances of this living world. My goal is to provide you with proof of an amazing conscious earth and your connectivity to everything upon her. Gaia, your earth, is the emerald planet--a planet of higher learning, a planet of great diversity and a planet of incredible beauty. The earth is a planet of free choice providing individuals with extraordinary experiences. Gaia is a planet that, when the human element upon her learns to live in harmony, will be an environment of great joy and adventure for the residents upon her and her future visitors.

Leni and I started this work by informing you about enormously powerful universal principles. We gave you insights into how you navigate through your varying lifestyles and how you could capitalize on your navigation. In a prior chapter I presented the concept that everything has soul. Webster's definition of *"soul"* is *"an immaterial essence of individual life...spiritual force; or the central or integral part of vital core...that which has essence or consciousness; a state of being."* On further investigation into the definition of life, Webster defines *life* as: *"...the quality that distinguishes a vital functional being from a dead body or inanimate matter."* And just to add a final element of definition, Webster's defines *consciousness* as: *"...aware, mentally awake or alert, done with awareness or purpose."*

In consideration of these definitions, would this awareness change your perception of the world on which you reside? Take into consideration the definitions and then ask:

1. Do I believe the earth has consciousness?

2. Do I believe everything has consciousness?

3. Would you like some proof?

Storms/Weather Events

For years I have been watching storms, their paths, the severity, and the type of weather event globally. I have pondered their conscious determination and the purpose of their steerage. For a moment I would like you to recall the HeartMath Institute experiments with Hubble referenced earlier. Their research documented emotional signals registered in space derived from the inhabitants of the planet's collective consciousness. How could Hubble register an emotional signal in space if consciousness didn't exist in space?

If the earth is a conscious planet that responds to the energies upon her, then doesn't it stand to reason that earth events (volcanic activity, earthquakes, floods, fires, tornadoes, hurricanes and the like) might respond to a conscious frequency? My answer and opinion is a resounding "Yes."

Consider the following scenarios and their potential impacts.

Yellowstone: Several years ago, the Yellowstone caldron's magma chamber (Yellowstone is a massive volcano) was building. A cry went out from Native American elders for light workers across the world to unite and lend their prayers to reducing the volatility of a pending eruption, an eruption that would destroy one third of the Northern Hemisphere spewing ash across the globe. This eruption could potentially cause a global winter. Lightworker prayers were successful in diminishing the magma base and for the moment preventing a pending eruption disbursing the core pressure to other fissures along planetary vents.

Repetitive Hurricanes and Potential Frequencies: Repetitive storm patterns serve as a warning mechanism to local residents presenting them with an opportunity to consider relocation. It was the summer of 2020 and four hurricanes plagued the Gulf Coast of the United States. While hurricanes along coastal regions are an inevitable event, four hurricanes directed at the same location might signal something more. What negative frequency could have fueled the pathway of the storms? The storm patterns were nearly identical, hammering the same cities and coast lines.

Years earlier there was a devastating oil spill in the Gulf that nearly annihilated a large portion of the Gulf's and the east coast's eco-systems, not to mention spoilage of the ocean's resources and stolen revenues from local businesses.

You might recall the Exxon Valdez catastrophe. This involved a massive oil leak when drilling penetrated the earth's crust one mile below the surface. This accident, by the way, required universal intervention (the galactic kind) to be able to plug the massive hole that penetrated the earth's crust. Human technology, at the time, did not have the knowledge or resources to be able to access the ocean depth to be successful in plugging the leak. Imagine if one of your major arteries was struck and you began bleeding. This is equivalent to the human medaling that was created by this accident for the sake of exploitation.

Poverty is another contributing factor that drew a lower magnetic frequency of thought. These thoughts were brought on by despair, anger, even violence, inequality and survival and may have acted as a potential magnet, thus drawing the negative pattern to the environment.

Storms and Their Purposes: Storms act as clearing vortices. While the storms inevitably cause destruction and damage to the human element, in its path there is ultimate clearing. Winds clear stagnant energies, clean the air, and usher in renewal. If storms have consciousness and are attracted to volatile frequencies representative of the energies present in that portion of land, then do you think your Light consciousness could reverse the damaging elements of a storm or provide steerage to send the storm onto a less damaging path? And again, the answer is a resounding YES. I must add here that you must ALWAYS ask permission from your Galactic Light masters before implementing any intervention. Once given permission (it's that little voice that whispers from within) follow the provided guidance to communicate with a specific storm's consciousness. This can provide you with the reason for the trajectory and the method to diminish the severity. Love usually becomes a miracle salve.

The Wisdom of Trees

We all know how protective any mom can be over her babies, but had you thought this might apply to the consciousness of trees?

In an earlier chapter it was suggested you might want to experiment with the energy of plants, acknowledging plants respond to sound, light, and your voice. But according to a Smithsonian article, (March of 2018) a *"Wise old mother tree will feed her saplings with liquid sugar and warn neighbors when danger approaches and begin to launch protective measures."* Wow! According to Peter Wohlleben (a German botanist), trees are connected to one another sharing water, nutrients, and sunlight. Furthermore, trees detect scent, experience pain when cut and send out electrical signals similar to the wounding of human tissue. They can sense danger and launch a chemical attack to discourage an intruder while warning surrounding trees of a pending onslaught.

Did you know trees provide healing? Have you ever hugged a tree or asked it to share its wisdom? You might be surprised at the response. I always ask permission before I trim or cut a tree and I provide protection for them before a pending violent storm.

I'm going to provide you with multiple YouTube presentations I will encourage you to investigate at your leisure. These will only provide evidence to support the theory of your conscious universe. Here is an excerpt from Peter Wohlleben's discoveries on the wisdom of trees.

https://youtu.be/1djibBPOfto

According to some extraordinary emerging experiments, trees can count, learn, and remember. What vast knowledge could a tree provide absorbing the experiences of its inhabitants over centuries?

Experimenting with Plants

We all know that plants provide us with medicinal properties, provide shelter, nourishment, and even clean the air we breathe.

Would you believe that plants emit sound? Experiments are currently underway to explore the healing properties of the resonate frequencies of plants that can shatter cancer.

What do you think plants sound like? The following is an excerpt from the experiments conducted by the Yale University School of Environment. Using a device called the "midi-sprout" students were able to extract the sound of plants. Here is a YouTube presentation on the research and sounds of plants.

https://youtu.be/8gPERvgAQTc

The Damanhur community has been exploring the ability to teach musical melodies to plants by allowing the plant to listen to the music and then replicate the sound. This certainly satisfies Webster's definition of soul and consciousness. And here is another interesting look with plants creating music.

https://www.youtube.com/watch?v=kuiUt91HeUg

Additional resources to explore include:

www.emeraldvoices.ca
www.wired.com

Since the initial research on plant synthesizers, many resources have emerged providing devices that use Bluetooth technology to connect through wireless systems to be able to reveal the sounds of plants. The technologies convert electrical impulses and use biorhythmic frequencies to extract the sound.

Some of the plant technology resources include:

- Plantwave.com, featured by NBC news and the New York Times. Unit pricing varies but currently are sold for $299 per unit.
- Plantchoir.com is another company selling a comparative device for $199.

I am certain that plants and our green elements satisfy Webster's definition of soul and consciousness.

The Insect Element

Nearly twenty-five years ago Machaelle Wright began experimenting with the idea of providing an insect garden to specifically attract insects to prevent the insects from feeding on garden crops. The insect garden was so successful not one crop was compromised. To showcase her experiments The Perelandra Nature Center was founded in 1995. Machaelle Wright expanded her research to provide essential oils, healing remedies for the land and has written many books on healing. Her work and the work of Perelandra can be further explored by visiting their website: www.perelandra-ltd.com.

This is just for fun. I must admit not all insects are endearing but I love to listen to the sound of crickets in the fall. Could the sounds of crickets provide something else? Once again YouTube will provide you with incredible intrigue with regard to our insect communities. Once you access YouTube, type in the search bar *"God's Cricket Chorus."* Take a listen to this natural phenomenon. Just to be clear, there are no human voices or instruments added. You are listening to the sounds of crickets slowed to a much lower sound frequency to reveal the hidden songs.

Animals and Their Healing Qualities

We all know how much we love our four-legged fur-babies. But have you considered how much love and healing they provide? Animals are integral to our living pleasures. Not only do they provide us with a familiar attachment but they assist as therapy companions in a multitude of specialties. They can be our eyes, our protection, a living extension of mobility, they can provide search and rescue, or provide ancillary services to hunters, livestock guardians, athletic pursuits and more.

I personally worked with Wounded Warrior therapy projects. I watched a young soldier who lost both his legs and one arm after a Humvee explosion, launch himself atop of a 1200-pound horse that adjusted its gait to help the warrior gain balance while the soldier was riding his noble steed. Horses chosen specifically for this program do not all have a calm demeanor, but they all seem to possess an inexplicable intuition that when caring for these special riders involved in therapeutic encounters express incredible intelligence and caring natures.

Another inexplicable account of the amazing healing therapy animals can provide can be viewed on YouTube by going to the website and typing in the search bar *Peyo*. Click on any one of the amazing videos. You may want tissues handy.

The Universe

As you can see there are multiple YouTube references to research. There are even YouTube presentations that allow you to explore potential planetary origins. Here is a link you might wish to explore.

https://www.youtube.com/watch?v=IQL53eQ0cNA

I have provided you with several different scenarios of your conscious sentient world. I hope this has left you uplifted, amazed and newly aware to continue your research into universal elements and perhaps personal discoveries that will help you uncover many more personal and universal mysteries.

Leni Morrison and Jilliana Raymond

Meditation - Your Conscious Universe

Leni Morrison

Get relaxed taking three deep clearing and energizing breaths. Surround yourself within a golden egg and breathe in the golden light that fills the space. Breathe in all that you are.

Call in your supreme "I AM" presence. Become aware of your energy body. This is your physical vessel, your body of light. There is nothing to change and nothing to do. Receive Divine clearing beaming to you now.

Know you can heal yourself and call forth this blessing now. Ask to be connected to the consciousness of Mother Gaia. Breathe in connection to the medicine of the stars. Ask to be connected to the central sun. Breathe in the light from the great sun. Connect to the cosmic dance of light. Breathe in life.

Ask to be connected to Sophia Gaia, the quantum universal mind. Breathe in wisdom, understanding and healing. Release anything that no longer serves you into the crystal heart of Gaia. Ask that anything that no longer serves you be purified in the molten heart of Gaia. Anchor your Avatar Consciousness into your physical body.

Breathe in all that you are, all that you have been, and all you will ever be. Allow the purity of your own light and holy essence to heal you now. Trust that you are becoming clearer and stronger than you have ever been before. Your sovereignty in this physical vessel is undefeatable. You are connected to the wisdom of the universe, all quantum fields. Here there is unshakable peace within you even when challenges arise.

Allow your light to illuminate all those around you. Call in more ability to heal yourself. Know you are expanding in truth and aligning with your pure essence. Breathe in the illumined diamond light.

Discovering Your Mastery

The new earth nurtures you even more deeply now. Your Source connection heals you. Release the ego body. Release the pain body. Release doubt, separation, abandonment, and fear.

Receive the purified light from the emerald codes and frequencies within you. Your new frequencies override all conflict, oppression, judgement and unforgiveness. Allow the great central sun to rise inside you. Allow the light of a billion stars to shine from within you. Your light and your power surround you.

Illuminate all shadows back into love, transmuting all pain.

Remember the future is bright and safe. Make the decision to be part of this golden age of light.

Know you truly belong here at this time now. Know there is no place in this universe that you do not belong. Know there is no moment in time or space that cannot sense or receive you.

Embrace the earth as she nurtures you always. Breathe in her essence. You are an illumined being here to share your love with those you touch. Know that you are something greater than you could have ever imagined.

Show gratitude for all your loved ones now. Live your life as a truly authentic being. Be the harmony you wish to see in the world. Know that each day you can renew your light, live in harmony, peace, and joy.

Solar Logos
Leni Morrison

The Glory of the Sun

INDIGENOUS CULTURES HAVE LONG REVERED THE SUN AS THE PINNACLE of heaven. Egyptians worshipped Ra (the sun god). Ra was believed to rule the sky, the earth and the underworlds. It was said Ra was born each morning in the East and died each night in the West. Other ancient sun cultures that established solar religions include Indo-Europeans and Meso-Americans. Aboriginal civilizations look to the sun for sustenance as do the First Peoples. The Mayans and the Aztecs worshiped the sun. Early Christian symbolism refers to Christ as the *"Spiritual Sun,"* the source of harmony and spiritual insight. Early Greek cultures believed the sun or 'Helios' (later known as Sol, its Latin moniker) had intelligence. The Romans believed the sun was the preserver of human life as well as the overseer of all the many kingdoms on planet earth. Since time began, the sun has been known as the beginning of all life and the essence of all light, perhaps this is why so many ancient cultures and keepers of the truth adored and revered the power of this giant golden star.

Glenda Green is an author and universal channel. In her book *"Love Without End, Jesus Speaks,"* the empath interprets the wisdom from Jesus as she explains: "If every human were to greet the first morning sun by activating each of their chakras so the sun would move through the breath into each open wheel of light in their energy body, and then do the same exercise just as the sun goes down, no one would ever be ill a day in their life." This is a profound message and a very powerful lesson for us to explore deeply. In my own quest for healing with light codes, I have found this sacred practice to be most invigorating and rejuvenating.

The Solar Logos

For many centuries, the cosmic wisdom keepers understood that the sun has the power to transmit its eternal soul intelligence from the Solar Logos to humanity. The definition of Solar Logos is multilayered but the aim here is to hopefully satisfy some curiosity about cosmic systems. So first, let's explain some definitions. Solar, naturally, refers to light, specifically light from the sun. The universe was created under two fundamental principles: one being *Love*, as the emotional component, and the other being *Light*, as the energetic sustaining component of all life. Logos translates as the word of God, the heart or Source of all creation. It also refers to the celestial design represented by the symbol of the sun. The Solar Logos represents the Light and Love of the creative design of a universal matrix and it charges the infinite monadic spirit and avataric soul matrices with immense power throughout the lower dimensions. It is responsible for helping the sun and all her inhabitants to ascend into the next harmonic universe. The "Ascension Glossary" (a website dedicated to ascension as directed by the Guardians) describes the Solar Logos as the Avatar Christos matrix. An avatar is an incarnate divine, spiritual teacher who is fully enlightened and can usually work miracles. The avatar frequency is the energetic reality of experiencing unity with God or Source. The Solar Logos holds the frequency bandwidths of the tenth, eleventh and twelfth dimensions in our universal time matrix. These higher frequencies contain unity intelligence. And this is where enlightened inter-dimensional contact connects deeply to the universal unity field of consciousness. The Solar Logos could be thought of as a giant universal generator as it has the strength to harness Cosmic Christ Consciousness on earth. 'Christos Avatar' is a term used to describe a higher dimensional conscious being that exhibits the purest expression of love; promotes harmony and holds the vibration of the diamond light. Avatar consciousness is what is required to help souls to ascend directly back into the Universal Mind and Cosmic Logos.

When all twelve DNA strands are awakened and activated by an infusion of both this diamond light and the emerald codes (which I go into more detail about later in the book), Cosmic Christ Consciousness and Avatar Consciousness are then generated and transmitted through our toroidal fields, thus assisting the sun and all the inhabitants of earth to ascend. And it is vital to note that humans are able to move through the universal star gates and gain access into the higher dimensions of reality, because they have the potential to embody Solar Christ DNA. In fact, the human body is a valued genetic solar technology, as humans have so many more abilities, emotional senses, and possibilities that exist in their physical body than they ever could imagine. We have been so blinded to our royal heritage and our divine blueprint. But thankfully, in this age of ascension, we are waking up to our sovereignty and freedom again. And, the aim of sharing this cosmic wisdom is to show you that you too can awaken your DNA markers. Through a combination of focused meditations and attention; deep prayer and decrees; connecting to avatar consciousness and calling out for assistance from the solar logos, you can achieve this—and many of these devotional practices are provided within the meditations and lessons within this book. We can, now, at this current time of bifurcation on ascending earth, completely transmute the karmic imprints, overlays, and distortions and move our souls into the higher frequency bandwidths through allowing this sun image as avatar Christos light, to heal all of our shadows for once and for all. Harmony on earth is finally being restored.

Early Christians believed the logos became activated on earth at the advent of the life of Jesus and that He took on the form of the Christed one to save humanity. This was an individual of deep wisdom, love and purity or a Christos Avatar who came to ignite Christ Consciousness on earth. An important note regarding the nomenclature of the "Christed" one, "Christos" avatar, or "Sophia Christ Consciousness," is that these are not references to religious identifications.

The terms apply to one who has attained the highest light vibration while in a physical body on earth. This can be seen as the auric field or the halo that is so often portrayed surrounding iconic religious figures. The "Light" represents the vibration of love and the activation of the divine genome.

Early Christians depicted Christ as the Spiritual Sun, the illumined source of order, the bringer of harmony and spiritual insight. If civilizations could have adopted the wisdom of enlightenment during the time of Jesus' human embodiment, the evolution of humanity would be far more advanced than it is currently. In a philosophical writing "*The Phenomenon of Man,*" Tielhard de Chardin proposed that if all creatures could exist in harmony with one another, as was presented through the word of Jesus, the Christ, then the Cosmic Christ personalities could connect throughout the cosmos. His belief was that Jesus, as represented as the Christos Logos was the "cosmic glue" of the universe. Another philosopher, Dr. David Fideler writes in his book *Jesus Christ, Sun of God: Ancient Cosmology and Early Christian Symbolism*, "all are Cosmic Christs, all royal persons of beauty and grace. But what good is this if none know this? Everyone is a Sun of God. We are all called, like the Cosmic Christ, to radiate the divine presence to and from one another." Some believe that it is not so much that Christ as one man will return to 'save us' but rather that we as a human race will awaken to our own royal heritage. Perhaps, it is through the gift of the cosmic, emerald and diamond codes sent by the solar logos and from Gaia, that humanity may finally realize that it is we who hold the keys and are the 'Christed' beings. That it is within humans to reclaim our divine birthright and it is time now that we stop waiting to be saved, but rather we step into our light, to become the saviors of ourselves. To herald the Golden Age, Lisa Renee (creator of the *Ascension Glossary*) reveals through her channeling and galactic study that "without the Solar Logos, the Sun and its many Soul Matrices would eventually expire and the Sun would not fully achieve ascension into the next Universe. The Solar Logos has the Source power to resurrect Solar Consciousness forms." She goes on to say that "Without the Solar Logos, souls would continue to descend into lower vibration and fragmented soul particles." The natural principles of harmony lie in the nature of the Logos. Harmony in nature is what binds us all in greater affection and deeper love and understanding for each other. To be in harmony is to be living within the principles of the Logos, where all are one and there are no divisions, duality or separation. When this is achieved, a higher evolved communication with Source and with advanced civilizations throughout the cosmos can be once again achieved. With this brief explanation of the Solar Logos we begin to understand the importance of the interventional energy coming to humanity from this giant spherical star. This grand universal support system is here to elevate each soul on earth through its transmission of light codes and frequencies designed to increase a vibratory field. These light codes provide a greater connectivity to universal resources and eliminate the chaotic fields and false timelines of individuals throughout the world and the universe.

Dimensions

Leni Morrison

It just seems appropriate that a discussion on spiritual dimensions would follow a discussion of the solar logos. Before an exploration of dimensions ensues, it might be relevant to provide a theory on the origin of the universe. In the beginning of all creation the resonant sound of OHM began to vibrate. Sound runs through all creation as depicted by the philosophic musings of Pythagoras. Current NASA investigations are exploring resonance frequencies and their association with the creation of cosmic origins. NASA is even conducting experiments on the moon with sound vibration. NASA has referred to the moon as a "giant bell," largely because of what is felt to be empty chambers that allow a sound vibration to reverberate throughout its energy field and resonate throughout the universe. What can this signal to civilizations as to the creation of the universe? There is certainly much research that remains to be conducted. In the chapter "Your Conscious Universe," there were references to sound depicted by the music of plants and insects. I suspect with further research there could be a link of connectivity to a much more diverse universe. In fact, there are several references to the varying sounds of planetary matrices online. This supports the theory that the origin of the universe began with harmonic sound. And interestingly, as you move through the dimensional fields, you move in octaves as you pass through the veils between the dimensional fields.

Dimensions

According to Galactic Channel and Interventional Shaman Lisa Renee, the chakra system in the body correlates to Gaia's universal dimensional system. When compared to symbolic resonance each chakra can conform to a dimensional level of energy and within each chakra you have a mind. The consciousness of humanity is inexplicably connected to the consciousness of the earth, as both the crystalline chromosomes in the new human, as well as the crystalline labyrinth of the earth, contain the emerald codes of ascension.

The first three chakras are associated with one's personality. Generally, these include the root chakra (foundation chakra), the sacral or second chakra (creative center), the solar plexus or third chakra (identity/egoic center). These chakras can be influenced by lower frequency intrusions triggered by fear, misunderstandings, electronic frequencies through the world's fascination with technology and communication through mobile and satellite devices. These magnetic frequencies can interfere with communication between solar resources and galactic intermediaries. In addition, individuals living within the framework of survival, continues to sabotage or block these chakra zones and perpetuate a lower vibratory dimensional resonance that continues to loop through eternity.

According to Lisa Renee this is likened to the First Harmonic Universe. Generally, individuals whose thoughts operate in the first three dimensional layers, experience what is referred to as the 'personality'. It is here in this dimensional reality (or mindset) that you eventually realize that all of life is an illusion…because this is where all duality and polarity exists. It is in this reality where individuals create identities to play with so that, on a higher/soul level, you can experience all the lower emotions, addictions, trauma, suffering and so on.

The second Harmonic Universe is linked to the 4th, 5th and 6th chakras. This is called the "Soul matrix", or the "Trinity Body". The heart chakra is connected to the soul matrix and allows you to begin to see your sovereignty. Once you move out of the disempowering stages of the first three dimensions you are able to access Christ Consciousness and you then begin to sense your Divine genome. Here is where the soul begins to recall soul fragments from lives spent in challenge and suffering. The toughest initiation of all is moving from the third dimension to the fourth dimension as you experience a tsunami of "shadow energy" or what is referred to as "the dark night of the soul." A shift in consciousness or realization that you are in control of your living experience can elevate you into higher vibrational dimensions but also deeply rock your world. So it is how you cope with this information that is important here.

A meditative practice, focused attention, pure presence, or calling upon the Solar Logos to help guide you through your life journey begins here. When called upon, this is where a team of illumined beings surround you to assist in advancing your vibratory frequency. Once in harmony and resonance with higher vibratory dimensions, you are able to access cosmic wisdom and receive energy infusions from photonic light streams.

In the third and fourth dimensions consciousness is massively reconfigured. Here old belief systems are completely dismantled. Hereto, the subconscious memories of prior ancestral overlays exist. Residual traumas from past or current presentations need to be cleared before any forward progress can be made. Here again is where the Solar Logos can be called upon to transmute tethered belief systems that no longer serve the higher vibrational dimensions. Once old belief systems and traumas have been balanced, released, or purified, connectivity to Christ Consciousness and higher dimensions like the Fifth Dimensional reality can be accessed. Some refer to the Fifth Dimension as the New Earth.

In the fifth and sixth dimensional levels exist realms of love and how to express yourself as a being of love. It is in this dimension that you have the **will** to act on the belief *that you are capable of achieving anything* once it is **heart aligned**.

The sixth chakra (the third eye located between your eyes) represents the chakra of insight. Ancient histories reflect upon the symbolism of the sixth chakra as the all-seeing eye. Current histories present the symbolism on our monetary exchange, in secret societies and in building structures, all emulating to revere something of a higher spiritual origin. This has been the dimension of guides and teachers, an intermediate dimension connecting both lower dimensional fields to higher vibratory realms of wisdom and guidance. According to Lisa Renee this dimension is referred to as the Harmonic Universe of the soul matrix.

The third dimensional body consists of the seventh, eighth and ninth chakras and corresponding dimensions. The seventh chakra is generally referred to as the crown. The eighth chakra is thought to be a connection point to Divine Light transmission. Meditation usually commences with a connection through this chakra allowing access to the higher cosmic vibratory fields. These chakra centers could be called the Over Soul matrix. This is called the Third Harmonic Universe. In this dimensional field you become aware of your multidimensionality and begin to design how you wish to experience your personal hologram.

The Avatar Consciousness fields consist of the tenth, eleventh and twelfth dimensional fields. This dimension is also referred to as the fourth Harmonic Universe. This dimension is the home of Master vibrations.

The Monadic Level of consciousness consists in the thirteenth, fourteenth and fifteenth dimensions. The veils of illusion no longer exist here. Star councils, angelic hierarchy, master souls reside in the higher dimensions. Here there is oneness in all things. This is called the Fifth Harmonic Universe.

Advanced galactic civilizations also exist on higher frequency dimensions as representative of their highly evolved civilizations. Earth has traditionally been a dimension of higher learning in a complex realm of imperfection. The higher cosmic and galactic frequencies emanating from these highly evolved civilizations, is what positively influences the frequencies of the earth. If the energy infusion and photonic light streaming is successful, then the earth and her living inhabitants can evolve, allowing for her transmuted frequency to move into higher dimensional residence. This can be correlative to a cosmic field of unity or unity consciousness.

The Emerald Codes

Leni Morrison

Activating the Emerald Codes:

ONE MORNING IN 2017, WHILE MEDITATING VERY EARLY, I SUDDENLY felt a powerful surge of light activating within my solar plexus. I watched as my entire center expanded outward like a warm sun. The energy, descending, brushed and enfolded me, with such pressure that I felt like I would implode. This sun-energy was like a radiant flash of photonic light—massive and unending as it poured into my body from high above. Then an almighty surge of energy began from the opposite direction; it pushed upward into my heart chakra and, with this activation, my whole being lit up like a million flashing stars of diamond light.

This was not the first time I'd experienced subtle energies. Ever since I was a very young child, I have learned how to be discerning. I used to experience how the room would fill up with energies. So much joy was felt in this special visitation (in 2017) that I had no doubt as to its original source: that of pure love and benevolence—so blissful and intensely magical that it suffused every subatomic particle of my being with the solar Christ consciousness: pure light. I experienced in this exchange a light that is clear and radiant, the diamond and emerald light, which can be called 'solar plasma light'.

Through the light codes, a message arrived instantly: 'You are completely safe and you are never alone. We are with you always, and we are helping you to heal'. During this light activation, I was shown my entire DNA structure and toroidal fields (spherical magnetic fields). Each strand of my DNA was being rewritten and recalibrated throughout. In later years, I knew this light infusion to be the activation of the crystalline chromosomes in my DNA.

Not long after this experience, I spent some time in Glastonbury Tor. It was only after I arrived there that I realized the purpose of my visit: to connect with a very powerful being of light. I somehow found myself meditating at a fountain and later praying within a small chapel and rose garden. It was here while praying, on an Easter Sunday morning in 2017 that I received the message to remember who I am. I was now to watch out for signs and to remember all of the signs that spirit had been sending me throughout my life. I received the message, too, that I must always follow my heart.

The divine feminine emissary of light is known as Mary Magdalene. It was she who communicated with me in the chapel and garden. The Magdalene revealed my life work and divine purpose to me, too. It was explained that a lot of women would be coming to me in the future. These women would share a similar karmic anguish as my own—carried over many lifetimes. She then imparted to me knowledge of the emerald codes. It was explained that they contain great wisdom and impact.

The emerald codes can be likened to a crystallized support system that runs through the whole of creation. This system is giant, universal, cosmic, elemental, biological, and ecological.

In the beginning of creation it is said that all humans incarnated with an emerald light, shining out from deep inside the secret chambers of their hearts. Did the Almighty and supreme Source of all that is place this emerald light there? And is this perhaps why our heart chakras are green? When awakened, these emerald codes play the role, I believe, of assisting us in healing, in a profound and transformational way. This healing penetrates every layer, level, and dimension of our being. And these codes are ubiquitous. They emanate from the new-earth grid of ascending Gaia. They can be found within waterfalls and mountains, as well as lakes and rivers.

The emerald codes are also found within the crystalline DNA and awakened hearts of the new human template. They stream, too, from the Great Central Sun, otherwise known as the 'God Star'. By 'new human template', I mean that our very nature and being is changing from a carbon base to a crystalline base energy. This is happening through the re-awakening of the 'God-particle' or Christ-conscious strands lying dormant within our DNA (as ascension markers). Once activated and embodied, the emerald codes assist in helping us to remember who we really are and what our divine purpose is, here on earth. We also realize that our main purpose, here, is to reunite with our Source again, with Mother-Father God, and with the light.

This reunification process, which can be felt by some, may be experienced as a rush of light and as ecstatic bliss, which immediately releases trauma, addiction, pain, and suffering from our cellular memories, as well as from our Akashic records. The codes also help to purge Mother Earth of her traumas, such as war and disease, held within her mantle. So, the codes also, therefore, greatly assist with healing and balancing planetary karma. The codes manifest in many ways—for instance through plasma transmissions from the cosmos and through photonic light waves and solar flashing from the Solar Logos. They also vibrate and travel via the frequencies of the electromagnetic field of Gaia—and within the crystalline chromosomes of our DNA. When we work consciously with these codes, we can be of divine service and assist with collective healing; we may help raise the earth's vibration by anchoring the cosmic Christ consciousness. So, you could say that ultimately the emerald codes assist with our spiritual ascension.

These next few short stories will outline how the emerald codes work in magical and compelling ways. As you will see from these stories, the codes can manifest in myriad ways, such as by symbols, signs, blissful internal rushes, or waves of light. You may experience an actual sensation of the crystalline chromosomes waking up inside of you. Messages from spirit and from the company of heaven will likely happen at the same time. Perhaps you will realize that you too are part of the great emerald awakening on Gaia. The idea behind these codes is very simple: As you clear and heal yourself, you then clear and heal the earth. We then ascend together in harmony.

As we are all one, and therefore, all connected, we participate in a unified intelligence and consciousness that exists all around us and at all times. I hope that these next few stories will show you clearly, that the emerald codes are like universal glue which binds by an attractive force. The codes allow the higher consciousness to evolve and greatly assist humanity. These stories will illustrate, in an enjoyable way, how the emerald codes are both very real within us and very present within all of creation. (The names have been changed to preserve their privacy).

John: Ask and You Shall Receive

John was going through an extremely agonizing time. The company he worked for was under fire for in-house bullying (the human resources department was involved). As one of the main victims, and as a sensitive empath, the harassment was crushing John's spirits. He worried that leaving this job would leave him and his young family homeless. In his city, you were only ever one pay-check away from such a fate. He couldn't sleep most nights; he felt that the world was crashing down upon him and ruining his lungs. His physical state was weak and anguished.

One night, while trying to sleep, he called out to Archangel Michael to send him protection. He meditated and visualized a huge diamond and sapphire shield all around his chest. The next day, he was overwhelmed, as usual, by the toxic energies in his building. On his lunch break, he went outside to sit in the park, where he felt utterly depressed. This was not the first time that he had faced unemployment, homelessness, eviction, or bullying. He was quite simply worn out.

The next thing that happened was incredible. To his absolute amazement, through his tears and pain, a crow swooped down and left an earring on his lap. The earring was a faux diamond and sapphire piece of jewelry in the shape of a miniature shield. John felt a 'rush of light' move through his whole system, accompanied by a blissful feeling of 'pure love' (as he described it). In this moment, his heart burst wide open and his emerald codes flashed awake! Help came quickly to his side.

John's anxiety completely disappeared. Then money came for his rent from various unexpected sources, and a new job followed the following week. The emerald codes, awakened through the prayer to Archangel Michael, gave him renewed hope and faith.

This is a powerful example of just how important it is to ask for help and to know that you deserve it. The universe wants to step in. The help may not come in the ways you would expect or at the exact time you call out for it, but it is coming. The more you let go of the human struggle and hand over your problems to the beings of light, the more easily and efficiently healing can happen. Just as water flows easily through and around an open hand, so does energy. But when you try to grab the water in your closed fist, it can neither flow nor be fully felt. Healing energy can be likened to water. So, once you ask, let it go and let it flow.

Marina: Past Life Healing

Marina was seven months pregnant and on holiday with her family in the Canary Islands (formerly known as Atlantis). It was a special time for them, as very soon life was about to change with a new baby coming. Marina was about to be a single mum. She was nervous about motherhood and often worried about her future. Most nights she wept silently while praying to the stars above. Her prayer was for her soul energies, once again, to restore her to her natural vitality.

One morning she was guided to leave her apartment and to find a church. She suddenly found herself (weirdly) in a shopping mall. She then heard the most incredible angelic voices singing within the mall. She followed the sound, which led her to a small church full of stained-glass windows. She timidly stepped across the threshold of a small evangelical church. Immediately, a million dazzling rainbow lights started streaming through the stained-glass windows. The combination of the angelic voices and the prismatic light shining onto her body immediately filled her with the most incredible 'rush of light'. Tears of ecstatic bliss were rolling down her cheeks and her entire body was bathed in this rainbow of illumination.

Marina was momentarily transported to a previous lifetime in Atlantis, where she had been a crystal healer. That life flashed clearly before her as she stood, once again, on the ley lines where her soul had splintered off many, many lifetimes before. Her DNA was immediately activated as the Akashic records opened. She remembered who she was! In that experience of light, she awakened the emerald codes within her. The part of her soul, which had once been left behind in Atlantis after the Great Fall, had now returned eons later to be reclaimed.

Marina had been crying out to the stars, requesting help for soul retrieval, for many months that year. But it was in this experience in a little church on the Canary Islands that her emerald codes flashed within her to reunite her with God and connect her back to her divine purpose: to be a crystal healer. She was meant to be an amazing, self-sufficient, empowered spiritual mama—and that is who she is to this day.

Leni: Soul Healing in Special Lands and Places

As a child, I had a recurring dream of being killed in the mountainous area of Sedona, Arizona. I always instinctively knew that I would, one day, go back to that location and reclaim that part of my soul that had split off and fragmented that day. On a cellular-spiritual level, I needed to return to make peace with the land where my DNA had undergone severe trauma. Upon opening my heart and initiating song and prayer, I could feel the emerald codes activating within me; now the karma had been released and undone. When I opened my eyes, to my amazement, the most beautiful Lemurian quartz crystal was waiting for me under my palm as I prayed. Sometimes, I like to imagine that an aspect of myself from the future left that gift on Cathedral Rock—just for me to collect once my Sedona soul work had been done.

Breda Morrison: Jesus with Diamond Eyes

When my mother was making her first confession at the age of seven, upon walking into the confessional she was unexpectedly greeted by Jesus. He exuded his Almighty presence and filled her energy field with light as they sat in the dark little box (which was the style of the confessional in those days). She recalls that Jesus had long hair. 'His eyes were shining like diamonds'. My mother was expecting the local priest. So she was kind of miffed that it wasn't him actually! Years later, when she finally met the actual priest who was supposed to be taking her confession, she was very unimpressed by how lacking he was in light and presence! I guess after meeting Jesus, it would be hard to hold a candle to Him.

My mother lost her own father when she was very young. Two sons passed away prematurely later on. She firmly believes that Jesus came to prepare her for the great pain ahead and to let her know that no matter what she would be okay. The company of heaven is always close by and, ultimately, she would always be watched over.

If in your life a great being of light comes to you, filling you with the light of God, the emerald codes are flashing and being activated. If you receive the blessing of heaven, it could be that your great inner strength is being shown to you. The message is that you are not to be afraid. Whatever happens to you in life, you will get through it with the grace of God.

Jim and his Mother: A Rose from Heaven

Jim and his mother were very devoted to St. Theresa of Lisieux and used to frequent a certain chapel. One day while praying alone in this chapel, in the front of the church a red rose came out of the tabernacle three times. Jim and his mother recalled how they were filled with light and their hearts opened. Not long after this experience, Jim's mother died, but Jim knew not to be sad, for she was in the rose garden with St. Theresa.

Molly and Maria: Akashic Records

Molly was a singer, doing a show in Las Vegas. She was getting her hair styled for the big show. Her assigned hairdresser was an Italian/American punk in her mid-50s. Maria was striking in appearance. As the two talked about the best style for the event, they felt a bond as if they were old friends. At the moment when Maria put her hands on Molly's head, they both 'left' the salon.

The two were immediately transported to a type of medieval courtyard. Maria suddenly noticed an unusual style of royal crown on Molly's head. Molly just felt the whole room change, as light came rushing through her body. Her heart burst open, and she was transported to another dimension. It turns out Maria is a very gifted medium and channel (as well as a part-time hair stylist). She understood from that experience that Molly had been a queen in Medieval Scotland. Molly really rocked her show that night, as she channeled her inner rock goddess and queen. The emerald codes, which carried their Akashic records, were activated as soon as Molly and Maria met and touched.

Saoirse: Angelic Heritage, Divine Purpose, the Visit of a Saint

Saoirse was on a holiday with a group of friends in Tuscany. As soon as she arrived she noticed a very strange atmosphere in the old farm house. This was later confirmed that very first evening when she spent the entire night communicating with a man who called himself Padre Pio. Saoirse vaguely remembered the name from childhood. In this visitation, he spoke to her as if they were old friends reconnecting again. They chatted long into the night.

Padre Pio told her all about his life. He had been a healer but no one believed in him and, as such, many doubted his gifts. He went on to tell her that he asked Jesus to help him in his plight. In answer to his prayers, Jesus Christ sent him his stigmata. This was to help Padre Pio prove his gift to the masses, and of course, this not only generated more popular interest but also, sadly, huge controversy.

The next morning, Saoirse got up to ask all her friends about Padre Pio and of course, they all knew who he was. She herself had hitherto forgotten about his existence. Besides explaining the power of healing, Padre Pio also talked about all the persecutions he went through after his stigmata experience.

For the rest of the holiday Saoirse and her friends happened to see Padre Pio reliquaries wherever they went. At the time of this appearance Saoirse was at a huge crossroads. She was uncertain whether to stay in the corporate world or to seek a new path. The visit with Padre Pio was a deeply healing experience. While Padre Pio was speaking, an intense rush of light ran through her and, at the same time, her heart burst open. Did this light from her heart mean that her emerald codes were flashing awake? Ever since this visitation she has allowed the gift of healing to flow through her naturally.

This event also triggered an old buried memory, which served to remind her of her own angelic heritage. Throughout most of her infancy and childhood, she had, in fact, spent her entire life with two angelic companions, though she kept this a secret. Two very large angels were flanked on either side of her. It was only after meeting Padre Pio many decades later that this memory rekindled.

Saoirse now remembers that she came to earth as a very pure being, and she firmly believes that Padre Pio appeared to remind her of her healing abilities. His role was to get her back in touch with her angelic presence and the codes within herself. Padre Pio was clearly a messenger directed to her from her angels. From that point on, Saoirse has continued to acknowledge their presence and to ask for their protection, guidance, and help.

Perhaps this story will remind you that you, too, have a deep bond to the Beings of Light and, in the knowing and trusting of that memory, you will once again allow your inner healer to shine on and reconnect you to your divine purpose on earth.

Peter: Forgiveness and Surrender

At nineteen Peter went through a harrowing, life-changing experience that left him scarred for decades. The horrific events unfolded after he was drugged by a group of idiotic teens. This painful episode led to his incarceration. This atrocious college 'misadventure' caused Peter to spend the next decade or more running away from people. He never stayed too long in a single place for fear that his dark secret would be exposed. But when a family member died he had to suddenly leave the remote island to which he had escaped and return home. It was at the funeral of his grandfather that a distant relative noticed his scarred appearance and battered soul. She said to him, 'Have you forgotten who you are? You were always so connected to the other side of the veil'.

In a moment of complete surrender and emotional release, Peter was suddenly reminded of his direct line to God and the angels. His heart burst open, his codes flashed, and his soul filled with the pure joy of forgiveness and purity once more.

This healing exchange with his long-lost cousin allowed for all his pain to suddenly wash away. Her words literally decoded his pain, and he finally remembered that he could surrender. He could just hand this pain over, as he was so weary of carrying it all on his own shoulders. In that instant, his once-fractured soul was reunited with his spirit and body, and it was by activating his codes that he could finally forgive his perpetrators for all the rapes and the abuse of the past. This cathartic clearing happened at the deepest level.

Through forgiveness, Peter healed not only himself but also the collective. This is how the codes work on a universal level. As you heal your pain, you heal it for others. Peter healed the abuse miasma for the world. The activation of the codes leads to a mass clearing for the earth and for all those who are ascension bound. The codes therefore reveal the truth: You are an angelic human and, as such, you are doing a divine service when you heal yourself. This is what unity consciousness is about on ascending Gaia.

The simple truth is that we are all connected, and once we release the trauma within us, the whole of creation gets a spiritual boost, too. By our own unique healing experience, our DNA gets upgraded and sends out waves of purity through the vibration of our toroidal waves. This spinning energy vortex out of our toroidal waves affects the electromagnetic fields within the crystals of the earth, too.

You could say that the emerald codes are here to help us ascend with Gaia. Through our compassion and forgiveness, we are set free and, in that freedom, the earth sings her song once more, because the divine feminine is once again re-birthed on earth. Through the heralding of the divine feminine, we finally get to release eons of sexual abuse and trauma on this planet.

I hope these stories have uncovered for you a basic new foundation for hope. We don't need to suffer anymore. The divine feminine is awakening through focused intention. We can be liberated from the false matrix. The message is clear. When you lead with the heart, you trust the light within you. By respecting the calling of your emerald heart, you and all of us get to ascend. In essence, we can bring heaven back down to earth. As angelic humans, our ultimate spiritual purpose is to assist this cosmic reunion.

Leni Morrison and Jilliana Raymond

Meditation - Emerald Codes

Leni Morrison

To anchor the healing energy of the emerald codes, close your eyes, take three deep clearing breaths and with each breath go deeper, becoming more relaxed.

Ask the universe to only allow pure radiant divine energies of the highest vibration to enter your vibratory field. Visualize a huge emerald rose opening above your crown chakra. Allow the light of the sun to ground deep into the core of the earth into the crystal heart of Gaia. Affirm you are releasing past traumas into the crystal heart of Gaia. Here they will be nurtured and loved back into pure light. Anchor in deep love, love of self, and love of your higher spirit.

Internally say: "Help me transform my deepest traumas into self-love. I am willing and open to fully release the past with love. I am embracing my multi-dimensionality into all realities now!"

I call back all fragmented parts of my soul now. I recognize my Divinity and call upon my higher conscious wisdom to manifest now.

I now command the Emerald Codes activate, activate, activate. Tap your heart three times. It is done, it is done, it is done.

By the power of three, I AM FREE.

For Your Contemplation

Jilliana Raymond

Choices

Throughout this work you've been shown how individual choices have played a significant role in how life is experienced. You've discovered that some choices were outlined long before you entered into a physical dimension. Often predetermined choices charted into your physical experience need to be played out in your physical experience. But many previously outlined scenarios can be altered. This revelation is the gift of the light codes and wisdom you are being presented within these pages. It is a gift sent to humanity through universal participation and an infusion of vibrational frequencies sent from our galactic neighbors that is lifting humanity into a new dimensional paradigm; one that offers the opportunity for those poised to embrace this opportunity with a life of harmony, joy, love, peace, wellness, and abundance.

Beliefs

In 2016 Dr. Bruce Lipton wrote a marvelous compilation on the *Biology of Belief*. The amazing research projected that varying belief systems determine how individuals walk through life and experience their living world. With this revelation how will you identify personal belief systems that may contribute to your life experience?

The hypothesis within Dr. Lipton's work is that thoughts shape your living experiences. Or to redirect this concept: that thoughts, more than likely representative of your beliefs, create those daily experiences throughout your life whether the thought is consciously projected or internally summoned from a subconscious belief. Your beliefs can be shaped from multiple resources; family expectations, a trusted friendship, cultural tradition, social expectations, an admired teacher or an internal revelation. Your true belief systems begin to surface when you can quiet your mind and look deeply into their origin to question whether their interpretations are actually your belief system or an inherited one. When you look beyond external influences you start to see what shapes your beliefs. You can then act upon your new insight from a fresh point of reference.

Understanding the Difference between Religion and Spirituality

With a new awareness of what shapes belief systems consider the following explanations regarding religion and spirituality and their differences. Being of "spirit" is not a religion. It is an essence, your essence. All earth inhabitants originate from a spiritual domain. All return to a spiritual realm. All have soul...a record keeper if you will that is your essence. Your true nature is that of a spirit. You are a spiritual composition regardless of what shape, character, gender, country of origin or religious preference you employ. You are spirit first having a physical experience.

While some may wish to assign a religious practice to the term "spirituality" it is certainly not a religion. It is an essence. I should also note that to be spiritual does not mean one belongs to a cult. One of course can belong to a devotee calling, but this falls under the category of a physical experience not a religious or spiritual calling. To be spiritual is a stand-alone experience.

Religion on the other hand is a chosen practice, perhaps a cultural tradition, with varying rules to participate within a particular house of worship. All houses of worship are recognized as sanctuaries where individuals congregate to be part of a family of worship. Nevertheless, while religious houses aim to promote love, harmony, forgiveness and peace they present rules of engagement within the specific orders of a specific organization.

There are no rules when describing spirituality. There are, however, more optimal ways to engage in life activities that exist within a spiritual framework. Universal guidelines help to steer humanity through a wide range of activities within the context of a planet whose fundamental energy exists within a template of free choice. To walk through life within a spiritual mainframe is to respect each individual's unique life expression without judgment. Every individual is expressing some element of physicality chosen to enhance that individual's soul's agenda. One individual journey may not be on your optimal list of experiences but there is some lesson or spiritual attribute the individual who is capturing your attention or disapproval has come to learn from that designed experience.

The Origin of Christianity

Would it surprise you to learn that Christianity has its origins in Judaism? The trend to be identified as Christian began around the first century AD following the crucifixion of Jesus of Nazareth. It should also be noted that the Encyclopedia Britannica defines Christianity as a religion.

The word 'Christed" comes from the Greek word 'Christos' or the 'anointed one.' This annotation is important to note because the term 'anointed one' is not a singular term but applies to any who has achieved the highest vibrational mastery. This attainment is usually visible, most notably from sacred images of the halo surrounding the Holy Mother as well as the halo representation surrounding the infant Jesus.

Many individuals have an ability to visualize the auric fields of individuals. Those, whose vibratory frequency is reflective of their life mastery, usually present with the same golden halo depicted on the images of the Holy Mother and Child. These individuals could be referred to as 'Christed.' The term 'Christed' then becomes an annotation of one's spiritual attainment and not a religious reflection.

Definitions of God

No matter whether you choose to be part of a religious practice or whether you choose not to believe in an omnipresent source, you are still part of a spiritual essence or soul. In fact, all reside within the matrix of a universal omnipresent (all-knowing) energy. None can ever be separate from this consciousness as you reside within the universal heart of God—not outside of it. God (or whatever preferred reference you wish to assign Source) is not something external, but internal. You can believe yourself separate from this benevolent energy, but you cannot be separate from it.

It took years of personal research before I was comfortable with a working comprehension of an omnipresent energy that millions of earth inhabitants identify with. It is understandable many would find resistance when providing a new perspective into the composite energy of Source.

Few cosmic resources can delineate the moment the universe was created and therefore a time when an omnipresent resource could be identified. As the universe has evolved, the concept of one energy source identified as God is the total resource of the grand universal design. A qualifying name for an omnipresent resource isn't necessary. God, Elohim, Adonai, Source, Great Is, Jehovah, Yaweh…all and more are names applied to an omnipresent resource. In some regions it is not acceptable to mention the name of God or have direct communication with an omnipresent Source. This couldn't be further from the truth. God is not some selective entity/energy that needs an intermediary to communicate on one's behalf. This is a manmade edict perhaps designed to provide allegiance of civilizations or to raise superiority to align the devotee to conform to the cultural belief customs.

God is neither he nor she. God is universal intelligence. It's part of every individual's DNA sequence where everything and everyone is connected to everything. Just to be clear, what many refer to as God is not something external but rather an energy that is innate to every conscious thing. If you have been paying attention, you reside upon a conscious planet. That means not only are you intrinsically connected to every living thing, but you are connected to the very consciousness on the earth you reside upon.

God has a conscious presence, a knowing--an all-knowing of every individual, of all events, all knowledge, but most importantly represents *ALL LOVE*. The concept of the universe was built on two energy aspects: **Light and Love.** What is God? God is Light—Solar Light. God is Love. God knows all suffering, all malcontent, all tragedy and uses an army of living angels to answer every call for help. It really is an impeccable system once you are aware of the blueprint.

While I'm on the subject of heavenly dynamics, St. Peter is not waiting at pearly gates to assess an individual's worthiness to enter heaven; you are. That's right, you and you alone stand in review of your life (and all preceding lives) to assess those life moments where perhaps you could have handled a situation differently. This isn't to say there is no accountability. Your soul is accumulating your life record and it is your soul's desire for you to evolve into higher dimensions to reach your ultimate potential. As such, it is your soul's aspiration that you physically want to satisfy. During your life review you will encounter those you have offended and those who have offended you. You will meet those you have helped and feel their gratitude. Within the spiritual ethers there is no judgement, no blame, no shame, and no guilt. There are, however, do-overs bolstered with a lot of love and guidance from those whose only goal is to see you achieve success, to reach enlightenment and to live your life in bliss.

Creating a New Paradigm

New choices offer individuals the chance to step out of limitation, to step away from tradition, to separate from outdated beliefs, expunge previously announced vows and to explore one's new aspirations. Belief systems from previous lifetimes can carry echoes from the past into current day life patterns. Looking deeply into internal reservoirs will expose life restrictions that may be running silently behind the scenes to compromise experiencing a life that is far more in alignment with a harmonious outcome.

There are a few constants to abide by when experiencing physical life. All are accountable for their individual choices and their resultant actions. Some individuals escape the karmic accountability when their energy frequency evolves to a level of harmony. Karma is disappearing as the evolutionary frequency of human life forms is accelerating. But for those who continue to live in separation and mayhem, karma is still very present.

Another constant is that all create the living conditions that become the daily lifestyles each becomes engaged in. While it may take some concentrated effort to change the daily déjà vu, anything can change. One revelation here is that as the earth accelerates in her vibratory frequency, individuals who cannot match her consciousness, who unfortunately seem resistant to change or whose vibratory frequencies are in too much contrast to the higher vibratory fields emitted by the new earth frequencies may not ascend into the 5th dimensional earth's new matrix. During their rebirth they will more than likely return to a 3rd dimensional earth and experience the karmic elements of transition until another evolutionary window of ascension appears.

How you live your current life on earth will largely determine how you will experience life in your spiritual house. While you may have endured many challenges during your present life, if your life is filled with compassion, harmony, and love you will experience harmony and an amazing adventure when you return to your spiritual house. If, however, your life is filled with anger, hatred, fear, the emotional baggage these characteristics create, these emotions can cause you to experience a more restrictive spiritual expression. A diminished life outlook also compromises a life expression that could be accompanied with joy and opportunity if the thought that created the disharmony cannot change.

Anything no longer in harmony or a vibrational match to every person, every location and every earth design that is in opposition to the intended living design in alignment with earth's ascension can remain.

Aligning With Higher Frequencies

Benefits and Discoveries

It is said that the universe began with the harmonic resonance frequency (aka sound). When sound began to vibrate, particle frequencies began

Discovering Your Mastery

to expand, and life was born. This is where the term vibratory frequency gathers importance. Everyone's energy frequency is determined by a vibratory frequency and that vibratory frequency is determined by thought. The ascending earth and the vibrational energies upon her are merging with more advanced planetary systems than our own in a cosmic rhythm of harmony and evolution.

Aligning with higher frequencies is definitely advantageous. The most prominent benefit is a profound insulation against disease with perhaps only the occasional cold. This isn't a frequency you can only sometimes embody…this is more a lifestyle that compliments the earth traveler to be a constant rather than a frequency you can only tap into momentarily.

Greater opportunities present for those incorporating a lifestyle that exists in harmony rather than that which exists in chaos and drama. Opportunity exists for those capable of incorporating change, change that will propel anyone into higher dimensions of living no matter what life station one employs. Your life foundation might have been in poverty, in sickness, in war. But no one can take from you a desire to resonate optimism, harmony, or love. The only way you can reside within a chaotic life stream is when you give your life opportunity and therefore your own personal energy away. Think for a moment how your vibration can change the environment in which you reside. One bright "light" (your energy) can light up any darkness.

It is disheartening that wars are declared in the name of religious supremacy or in declaration of land ownership, belief system, cultural separation or any other definition designed to separate individuals from living harmoniously upon this beautiful emerald planet. In the eyes of a Divine heart there is no designated religious supremacy. To live within the heart of God is to live in harmony with all surroundings. This does not mean you will engage with all equally, but it does mean that you will respect all beliefs, all presentations, cultural traditions, customs, and character variations, as all are expressions of Source.

It's time to shed an old egoic personality filled with society labels, identities, and restriction. It's time to emerge to the Divine Light you were intended to be. Go within…meditate, discover who you really are. The richness of your spirit is phenomenal, but you will need to engage in your own personal exploration to discover your true essence. Reread the wisdom within these pages. Discover your true spirit, not some identity that is superimposed upon you from society, cultural and familial designs.

Creating Your Spiritual Residence

How would you like to experience your presence within your spiritual residence? If the ideation of rebirth is not yet comfortable for you, ponder its potential just for a moment. Your soul is eternal. Death is not an end but the demarcation point for a new beginning; a life to be experienced in spiritual residence without diminished lifestyles, without suffering, or without limitations. Spiritual life can be whatever you wish to make it. Discard old belief systems of restriction and suffering. Embrace happiness and abundant opportunity. And relish the legacy of your accomplishments, no matter how insignificant you believe they may be.

New Earth Roles

As souls evolve, the earth environment is changing. New technologies offer advancement for humanity, an environment that will soon seem fresher and more alive. I'm talking about a harmonic energy that will allow inhabitants to respect cultural differences. In a new earth reality political beliefs don't matter. Cultural beliefs don't matter. Gender roles don't matter. Religious beliefs don't matter. The color of one's skin doesn't matter. The country of your birth doesn't matter. The only thing that matters is your spiritual evolution, how much wisdom you accumulate during your life experience, how you were treated and how you engage with all earth neighbors.

Children today are far more connected to a higher consciousness than any prior generation. These children are bringing change and advancement to humanity. They will revolutionize and dismantle any ideation of an archaic structure. You can see the energy reflected through their eyes. They may at times seem more defiant, intolerant of restrictions imposed upon an evolving humanity. The change these soul travelers provide will continue to raise the new earth's vibration to anchor the earth into a new stellar alignment more complimentary to the higher living dimensions of many galactic neighbors.

New environmental codes will be revealed. Better ways of living will be forthcoming. Farming enhancements are a threshold about to unfold. Cooperation between countries will become not only a necessity but a reality. Restrictive borders will soften. Old cultures of control will crumble. It may take some time, but a new earth reality is unfolding; one that serves all life with equal opportunity, understanding and harmony.

All play important roles in weaving life tapestries. Think about this for a moment, your life legacy (every life legacy) leaves a footprint in time, forever etched upon the earth. What vision can you provide for a new earth template? How would you like to live your life? Your life on this earth is your legacy. What will you have it reveal?

Universal Matrices

Finally, if you can embrace the ideation that our partnership with universal neighbors is evolving, then as the vibratory field of the earth's frequency is increasing, so too is the frequency complimenting other planetary systems within the galactic composition of the earth's universe. As the earth moves into higher dimensional fields within the universal matrices, our technological capabilities also become enhanced. This provides advancement to medical interventions, longevity of lifestyles, freedom to experience travel adventures without restriction, greater exploration into ancient histories of the universe and a harmonic connectivity to not only cultural neighbors but galactic systems as well. The exploration of our futures is enticing. How you will engage in future activities largely depends upon how you can embrace your life roles, living your physical life with a firm understanding of your spiritual essence.

About the Authors

Meet Leni Morrison

LENI MORRISON, B.A, E.C.C.E, P.G.C.E.

Leni is a fully certified Awakened Academy Spiritual Life Coach, Vibrational Energy healing Practitioner, Musician & New Earth Ascension Guide with a sharp Irish wit and charm, a talent for joy, and a secret penchant for peanut butter and banana sandwiches.

Her spiritual journey accelerated while living among shamans, sages and extraordinary humans in South America in her early twenties. It was here that she encountered many magical experiences and profound awakenings.

Leni sees clients of all ages from all over the world and leads weekly guided meditations with her 'Ascension Group' and 'Spiritual Healing Group' on MeetUp (via zoom) https://www.meetup.com/meetup-group-RIwSGzeI/

For more information on how to book a unique Gold Print Session with Leni, please check out her website: www.lenimorrison.com

Meet Jilliana Raymond

Author, speaker, spiritual teacher, energy channel and healing master, Jilliana Raymond has been introducing individuals to the spiritual stewards who watch over us through her writing and teaching for over 25 years. In 1990, Jilliana began researching the energy components that contribute to individual life events in search of answers to her own life challenges. She has studied with life masters and world class healers in pursuit of the wisdoms she shares with her audiences.

She is an international award-winning author, national radio guest, and webinar host distilling her discoveries into the powerful principles she explores through her writing and workshops, each designed to empower individuals, promote healing, and provide a greater understanding of the language and teachings of our spiritual universe. In addition, Jilliana is a National Board of Massage continuing education provider and healing master. Her healing toolbox includes therapeutic reflexology, craniosacral alignment, violet flame infusion and healing with the masters.

Research Credits

The following are websites and credits to contributing resources.

https://www.anandavala.info/TASTMOTNOR/TCOTCC.html

https://www.auroraorchestra.com/2019/05/28/pythagoras-the-music-of-the-spheres

https://www.britannica.com/topic/sun-worship

https://youtu.be/8gPERvgAQTc

https://youtu.be/1djibBPOfto

www.emeraldvoices.ca

www.perelandra-ltd.com

https://www.youtube.com/watch?v=kuiUt91HeUg

https://www.youtube.com/watch?v=IQL53eQ0cNA

www.wired.com

David Cousins/*Handbook for Light workers*

For those following a spiritual path, this guide attempts to supply answers regarding the new energies entering the planet with easy to follow advice.

Tielhard de Chardin/*The Phenomenon of Man.*

This is a dissertation on Logos and Christ Consciousness. https://en.wikipedia.org/wiki/The_Phenomenon_of_Man

Dictionary of Science – Explanation on toroidal fields.

Dr. Wayne Dyer

The author of multiple books on practical psychology, Dr. Dyer was a renowned author and speaker in fields of self-development and spiritual growth. His research provided spiritual aspects on the human experience. In his words, *"we are not our country, our race or religion. We are eternal spirits. Seeing ourselves as spiritual beings without a label is a way to transform the world and reach a sacred place for all of humanity."*

Dr. Masara Emoto/Messages in Water

Masara Emoto was a Japanese Doctor of Alternative Medicine. Photographs of his experiments were first featured in his book *Messages from Water* which became a best seller. Dr. Emoto became a pioneer in his study of water and his proof that thoughts and feelings affect physical reality. By producing different focused intentions through written and spoken words, water samples appear to change their expression.

Andre Ferrella/The Spirit Artist/www.andreferrella.com

Visionary Artist, Spiritual Engineer, and Multimedia Architect. Andre Ferrella has been a seeker inspired to use art to express spirituality and the Divine. Andre has sought, studied, and embraced the inter-connectedness of the universe from the microcosmic to the macrocosmic with the *Discovery of The Living Picture*. https://www.andreferrella.com.

David Fideler, PhD/*Jesus Christ, Sun of God: Ancient Cosmology and Early Christian Symbolism*

Dr. Fideler has worked as an editor and book publisher, a college professor, an educational consultant, and the director of a humanities center. His writings now explore questions that incorporate exploration on how to live life more dynamically.

M**atthew Fox**/*The Coming of the Cosmic Christ*

Matthew Fox is a spiritual theologian, an Episcopal priest presenting new concepts of understanding into the religious and spiritual myths and beliefs.

Mahatma Ghandi

Mohandas Karamchand Gandhi was an Indian lawyer, anti-colonial nationalist and political ethicist, who employed nonviolent resistance to lead the successful campaign for India's independence from British rule, and in turn inspired movements for civil rights and freedom across the world.

Glenda Green/*Love Without End, Jesus Speaks*

Glenda Green is one of the world's leading teachers of contemporary spirituality. Her teachings are directed toward universal truths that are uplifting and enlightening to all people of all beliefs.

HeartMath Institute - Doc Childre Founder

In 1991, Doc Childre founded the nonprofit HeartMath Institute, a research and education organization. HMI's educational and clinical research on emotional physiology and self-regulation has been published in peer-reviewed scientific journals and presented at many scientific conferences worldwide.

Jovian Archive/Ra Uru Hu/Human Design

The Human Design System is a synthesis of ancient and modern sciences proven to be a valuable tool for human understanding. The design template becomes a simple navigational tool to eliminate personality resistance and stress personal conflicts can create. The founder, Ra Uru Hu, received his knowledge in 1987 and dedicated his life to develop this comprehensive system. The BodyGraph illustration provides a distinct picture of the personal energetic flow within your system and a blueprint for how you interact with the world. Visiting the Jovian Archive website will give you access to acquire your own free human design template.

Bruce H. Lipton/*Biology of Belief*

Bruce Lipton, is an American developmental biologist notable for his views on epigenetics. In his book The Biology of Belief, he claims that beliefs control human biology rather than DNA and inheritance.

Dan Millman/*Life You Were Born to Live*

Utilizing birth date analysis this work reveals individual life purposes and becomes an ultimate resource for understanding personal characteristics. The origins of the system may date to the Pythagorean School of ancient Greece.

Carolyn Myss/Sacred Contracts

Caroline Myss is an American author of numerous books and audio tapes, including five New York Times Best Sellers: Anatomy of the Spirit, Why People Don't Heal and How They Can, Sacred Contracts, Invisible Acts of Power, Entering the Castle, and Defy Gravity. Each unique work provides character studies to assist in life navigation.

Smithsonian article, (March of 2018) a *"Wise old mother tree"*

Brian Weiss/*Many Lives, Many Masters*

Brian Weiss is an American psychiatrist, hypnotherapist, and author who specializes in past life regression. His writings include the studies of the past life regressions from client histories uncovering detailed encounters from past and future life profiles. His research ultimately documents proof of life beyond death.

Jim Woodward/Wired.com

Jim Woodward is the mind behind the website, the magazine and the concepts explored in relationship to the revolutionary hypotheses presented. Check out Wired.com to discover more on Gravity, Gizmos, and a Grand Theory of Interstellar Travel.

Glossary

Akash/Akashic Records/Akashic Stream – A compilation of life events throughout time and universe.

Archangel Gabriel – Angel of high hierarchal order traditionally associated with the energy of love. Biblically Gabrielle is noted to be a messenger.

Archangel Michael – Traditionally Michael is known as the angel of resolution, one who resolves conflict. Biblically Michael signifies one who is "like God."

Archangel Raphael – Raphael is known as the Archangel of healing.

Archangel Uriel – Angel of wisdom and faith.

Atlantis – Typically regarded as an advanced ancient civilization described by Plato.

Avatar - Any incarnation or embodiment, as of a quality or concept in a person.

Babaji – Babaji has been called an avatar. He is credited with working with Jesus to plan spiritual salvation for his era. The communion between Babaji and Jesus was to send out vibrations to inspire nations to renounce wars, racial hatreds, and counter materialistic ideations.

Bell Curve – The bell curve is a scientific registry of natural distribution involving many situations; a projection of outcome.

Christ Consciousness – The highest state of spiritual consciousness, emotional balance, wisdom. The term does not coincide with religious tradition when referring to Jesus as Christ. It is an attainment of truth and the evolution of becoming a living vessel of love.

Christed - Individuals who embody the highest vibrational frequency.

Cosmos – Simply means the universe.

Creator/God/Great Is/Source – The terms are endearing to reference a Source of light that from a quantum physics qualification emits an intelligent energy and source of life.

Crystalline Earth Grid – The power source that sustains earth frequencies.

Crystal Singers - A person whose vibratory capacity is sufficient to bring in cosmic sounds and to translate those sounds vibrationally through the etheric versions of their physical body on inner planes.

Divine Neutrality - The term applied in working towards unity, not separation, consciously releasing polarity, entering into exchanges without being pulled into one side or another, neither left nor right, being nothing and everything in your conscious co-creations with others. This is a compassionate detached state and represents the state of the pure solar cosmic Christ. It is staying calm and centered no matter how emotionally distracting energies surrounding us become.

DNA - A self-replicating material that is present in nearly all living organisms as the main constituent of chromosomes. It is the carrier of genetic information.

Embody - When an individual's DNA field is activated with unity consciousness the individual begins to experience an expanded energy field that radiates diamond-solar plasma light. When this happens, lower timelines fall away, and higher realities appear.

Emerald Codes - The higher vibratory field of radiance sent from the crystal heart of Gaia. Frequencies are being sent from universal ethers to assist humanity in activation of their Divine genome. These codes are energetic imprints held both in DNA and the ascension consciousness of Gaia. The connection between these energetic imprints is raising the vibratory signature of humanity.

Fall – References the fall of Atlantis in this instance.

Faery Rocks - Quartz rocks covered in silver flecks.

Gaia/Tara – Tara was an ancient name given to the earth during the era of Lemuria and Atlantis. Gaia was the ancient name given to earth at the time of earth's rebirth after the sinking of Lemuria and Atlantis.

Galactic Council - The Galactic Council is a coalition representing thousands of intelligent biological species. They are a peacekeeping force first and foremost. The Galactic Council negotiates non-aggression pacts between its various member worlds.

Ghost - An apparition of a dead person which is believed to appear or become manifest to the living.

God Star – The Central Sun.

Golden Age/Era - The earth is now positioned in the galaxy in the 5th dimension where life forms upon the planet will experience harmony, unity consciousness, love and all its diversity for an epic 2,000 years.

Heart Centered – An ability to be spiritually aware, yet able to live in a physical reality without compromising who you are.

Karuna Compassion - Karuna love is the medicine of unconditional compassion.

Kryon – Kryon is an angelic force working with the magnetic grid of earth's matrix. Their emergence in the 1980s has served to provide steerage for humanity during the transitional earth shift into the higher dimensions.

Lemuria - According to *The Lemurian Connection*, the history of Lemuria goes back to 4,500,000 BC, when the civilization ruled the earth. The continent of Lemuria was located in the Pacific Ocean and extended from western United States and Canada to lands in the Indian Ocean and Madagascar.

Light - An electromagnetic energy created by multiple frequencies. Various color spectrums delineate the dimensional quality of the energy. Light travels on quantum waves of energy.

Lightworker - A Lightworker is a person here on Earth for a reason. Every Lightworker usually has had a challenging life. This was part of their training to understand the polarity of darkness. Lightworkers have the capacity to change the world. They vibrate on high frequencies and are able to assess the energy of others with ease. They may be known for their healing skills. There work can be categorized into eight classifications:

1. Gatekeeper: Individuals who ensure love is infused throughout the world.
2. Healer: Enable higher frequency healing to transmute physical and emotional pain.
3. Messenger: Individuals capable of delivering important messages to their surrounding realm. They can boost the vibration of mankind. These individuals can be public speakers, life coaches, artists, writers, musicians.
4. Seer: Intuitive able to provide futuristic insight.
5. Neutralizer: Have an innate ability to stabilize compromising situations turning events into positive outcomes.
6. Dreamer: A transformational projector.
7. Adventurer: Individuals searching for something new, something better, and bringing to light a better future for all.
8. Manifestor: Individuals are usually spiritual leaders/teachers presenting information to help others achieve their goals.

Love - The highest frequency of light that aligns with truth, higher knowledge, and compassionate force. The fundamental frequency of life existence.

Mahatma Light – (meaning "Great Soul") Mahatma Light is an energy that indicates the highest and purist light any individual can assimilate.

Metatron - He is variously identified as the Prince (or Angel) of the Presence, as Michael the archangel, or as Enoch after his bodily ascent into heaven. His legends are predominantly found in mystical Kabbalistic texts.

Monadic - an individual substance which reflects the order of the world.

Phoenix Child - The term applies to an individual who realizes their sovereignty to love and be loved unconditionally. It is a term applied to the resurrection of the inner child that rises from the holy flames of the sacred heart.

Photonic Light - Ascension codes travel on light frequencies, also referred to as "living light." It is a Source-encoded intelligent light that sends light messages to the cellular body. Photonic Light works with the Solar Logos to provide crystalline plasma to cellular structures. Accelerating energy fields through coherent fields of harmony and love accelerate access to the photonic light streams.

Pleiades – The Pleiades are also known as the Seven Sisters, an open star cluster in the northwest of the constellation Taurus.

Pleiadians are known for their work with life forms. Pleiadian dolphins are an intergalactic star being who are assisting Earth and mankind in ascension.

Polarity - The quality or condition inherent in a body that exhibits opposite properties.

Quan Yin – Ascended Master working with all souls on earth who ask for assistance in alleviating pain and suffering. During her life she was subject to horrific trauma and pain. Her entire family was tortured by a marauding army. She was thought left for dead but beforehand was raped and mauled. She alone escaped her village to find safety in a distant forest. Because of her extreme trauma during her physical life her permanent home has become her spiritual residence.

Babaji spent many years assisting Quan Yin in overcoming her trauma and reclaim her soul light. He explained to her that she only had one lifetime on earth as she chose the most difficult life experience. Her suffering would make her a powerful asset to assist in resolving humanity's suffering.

Quickening – Massive groups of souls awakening to the ascension process through sudden accelerated evolution, it could be likened to a set of unique instructions or codes awakening large groups of soul clusters or star children at the same time, helping them to remember at once their mission or their divine birthright.

Resurrection Codes – These are codes stored within your DNA and accessed through your sacred heart by giving your inner consciousness permission to free yourself from ancestral stories from the past.

St. Germain – St. Germain is a legendary spiritual master of ancient wisdom in various theosophical teachings. He is said to be responsible for the New Age culture in the Age of Aquarius.

Seraphim - Angelic order, regarded in traditional Christian angelology as belonging to the highest order of the celestial hierarchy, associated with light and purity.

Shaman - A person who acts as intermediary between the natural and supernatural worlds.

Solar Christ Consciousness – This is a state of illuminated consciousness that embraces the union of all duality in human form. It is the transformation of identity from the individual self to the embodiment of universal love (Divine Feminine) and light (Divine Masculine). *http: Graceofthefemininechrist.*

Solar Logos – Eternal soul intelligence transmitted through the sun to humanity. A term applied to those who have achieved illumination. This is an individual who has achieved loving cosmic wisdom to aid in spiritual ascension awareness.

Solar Plasma Light – The result of diamond/emerald light infusion.

Soul Particle Retrieval – The healing of soul fracturing from past or present traumas.

Source – New thought term to reference an omnipresent energy more familiarly known as Yaweh, God, Jehovah, Ali, Mohammad, etc. It is a term that applies to an all-knowing intelligent energy.

Sovereignty - Supreme power or authority.

Spirit - Your vibrational essence. That part of you (soul particle) that connects your heart to your reality.

Star Gateway - This is the stellar gateway to Source, the connection point of the 12th chakra. The color is pure gold, the access point to receive divine energy. This gate can either be open or closed determined by the vibrational frequency expressed. This chakra holds the sum of all your experiences held in the twelfth dimension. It is your divine spark and the truest essence of who you are. Metatron is the seraphim that overseas this chakra. This is the access point to your Akashic Record. *(consciousreminder.com)*

Star seed - The term star seed refers to souls, spirits, and conscious beings that have come from an alternate world to help planet earth in some specific way. Their deep connectedness with the spiritual plane and access to ancient knowledge can inspire positive realizations amongst human beings.

Still Point/Zero Point – The energy field where time and space are absent. This is a unified field, a Source field state wherein creation is manifest.

Sun Source – Origin of primary energy.

Toroidal Field - A magnetic field where the magnetic lines of force lie on an electrically conducting spherical surface.

Universe – The cosmos in which earth is one of the planetary systems.

Zero Point - State of acceptance, surrender and love.

Author Resources

Leni Morrison

Contact: lenimorrison5@gmail.com
Web: www.lenimorrison.com
Calendly.com/lenimorrison5
https://www.meetup.com/meetup-group-RlwSGzel/

Many years of training, research, and dedicated practice in energy healer, as a multidimensional soul coach and ascension guide, have prepared Leni Morrison, Irish born educator, song writer and recording artist to provide cutting edge, light-infused healing sessions to her growing number of international clientele.

Leni's many accomplishments include degrees in Philosophy with a B.A. Honors Bachelor's Degree from the University of Dublin, a Master's Degree in Education from the University of Wales, a Diploma in Media and Communications from the Progressive College in Dublin, as well as I.T. Carlow Television Presenter Training, Presenter studio London Song Writer and Recording Artist, New York, London and Dublin. In addition to her many accomplishments Leni is a fully certified Life Coach, Vibrational Energy Healing Practitioner and Ascension Guide.

She now adds webinar presenter and authorship to her many universal talents. She conducts new earth courses, webinar programs on ascension, and weekly meditations.

Her galactic and quantum-based work will appeal to those souls who are either already on their ascension path or beginning their ascension journey. Individuals are deeply aware on a soul level that they are *Star Children*. These awakened beings need great support in helping them connect to their lineages, divine blueprints, and help with remembering their true purpose on earth.

Leni's wish is to be able to give the deepest support, wisdom, and guidance to this particular group of souls who may at times feel lost in the current earth energies. These individuals will benefit enormously from the DNA activations, the multidimensional courses, the Emerald Code infusions and her weekly meditations. This type of energy work involves the transmission of vibrational light codes which are transferred through her voice, her hands and through her heart field.

The energy activations are light-encoded and transmit energy codes and healing messages. These energy transmissions awaken the energetic systems and many intricate vortices of diamond and emerald light codes within the crystalline light body.

Among her many interventional capabilities include:

- Spiritual counselling: Her main areas of care are trauma, belief re patterning, addiction, self-love, depression, abandonment, toxic relationships, and separation.
- Soul Coaching: Helps in accessing gifts, instilling empowerment to discover hidden talents that were hitherto unseen.
- Soul retrieval: Returning fragmented soul particles to align with the complete soul embodiment.
- Ancestral trauma purification.
- Emotional Code work: Activation of DNA pathways to initiate the highest version and life potential of each client.
- Akashic record retrieval, breaking vows, curses, entity release.
- Conducts full etheric body scan to address energy distortions, imprints, overlays/tears in the auric field.

- ➢ Can detect blockages/impurities, underlying issues in organs, blood resources, bones and the physical body.
- ➢ Provides innovative light activations including Emerald Code activations.
- ➢ Accesses higher self-connectivity and multidimensional alignment, including re-patterning and DNA coding to include crystalline coding.

Consultations: For your first session we will work on the most pressing areas of the client's *'soul picture'* (i.e. energy blockages, physical, emotional, spiritual pain etc.) After the initial session, the number of follow-on sessions depend on the unique blueprint of each client. Bespoke healing packages can always be worked out.

Testimonials:

"Leni weaves a rich tapestry of spiritual channeling, life experience and innate truths, delivered with compassion, humor and absolute conviction". John L.

"Leni's words not only beautifully guided me through some life-changing meditation experiences, but helped me remember so much about myself & life" Florencia Rios Ortiz

''I had the pleasure to meet this Beautiful Angel, Leni, 2 years ago and it has made a wonderful impact in my life. Besides being an excellent professional, she is able to reach to you and read you in a way no one has managed before. Leni has an enormous heart and an unique touch of laughter. Every time I learn something new when Leni does her meditations/one to one healing work etc., the sensation of peace that I get is magical. I learned how to see and follow my own believes and not the ones the others try to input in me. I am always exited to hear that there is another course on its way (I did already a few with Leni), now I am even more exited with the release of her new book. I wish you Leni from my heart all the best. (Let it be the first of many books)'' Manu R.

"Leni Morrison's description of her own light body activation in 2017 is a fascinating introduction to the emerald frequencies, the Cosmic Christ, Gaia and humanity's somewhat messy, yet somehow magical ascension process that we now find ourselves in. One can breathe a sigh of relief as we follow her detailed explanation of how the transformation of our human DNA from carbon base to crystalline leads to blissful states of well-being and creative expression. The powerful awakening stories included in this chapter reveal how Source transmits plasma and photonic light waves that activate and support our embodied ascension process in unexpected and miraculous ways. Her writing emanates an authenticity that can only come through personal experience and deep work with the Emerald Codes. A great read for anyone in the midst of waking up to their own multidimensionality and Christed Self." ~Ana Estrada, Quantum Light Practice

Author Resources

Jilliana Raymond

Contact: jillianaraymond@gmail.com
Web: jillianaraymond.com

Trained by multiple life masters, world class energy healers, spiritual avatars, Jilliana uses the accumulated wisdom to assist others on their life transformational journey.

Energy practitioner, trained in multiple energy therapies to include:

- ➤ Therapeutic reflexology (Integrated Sole Energy Therapy): Unlocking congested energy corridors within the body allowing the body to initialize healing modalities.
- ➤ Craniosacral alignment: Realignment of the atlas and body alignment through energy transference.
- ➤ National Board of Massage Continuing Education Instructor.
- ➤ Spiritual minister who conducts spiritual life solutions utilizing spiritual understanding and simple energy techniques to release compromising energy systems from blocking joyful life navigation.
- ➤ Provides universal understanding of spiritual guardians and how to solicit intervention.
- ➤ Webinar presenter, providing multiple instructional courses to enhance individual knowledge of their connectivity to a spiritual universe.

- ➢ Transformational and award winning author to include *The New Covenants; Before Your Last Breath; New Beginnings; Life is a Spiritual Soup; God's Toolbox; How God Answers Prayers, I Hope Your Turkey Burns*; and co-author *Wake Up Life the Life You Love*. Titles available on Amazon.

Her life research has helped hundreds transform their lives, to experience a life that incorporates accelerated freedom, to live without emotional baggage and begin to thrive with new found knowledge, energy tools without compromise.

Spiritual consultations available in-person, via Zoom, through phone or internet. Therapeutic reflexology/craniosacral sessions by appointment. Continuing in-person education courses available in advanced therapeutic reflexology. See webpage for scheduling: www.jillianaraymond.com

Testimonials

"Knowledgeable and informative, I would recommend Jilliana without hesitation. She is an interesting and highly qualified speaker." Nathan Coles, DC

What if you could change your life in any way you want? Do you have a life purpose? How can you know? How can you find out? Can one person, one soul have more than one life? When people talk about "spirit", what do they mean? When I do my best to live a good life, why do bad things happen? How can I make my life better? Happier? I have heard that everything is energy. What does that mean?

Sometimes I hear voices or thoughts in my mind and wonder if I'm crazy… am I? Sometimes when I meet someone for the first time I feel like I've known them forever. What's up with this? Sometimes I feel like my dreams are real; are they? Sometimes I feel like I don't quite belong here, on this earth, at this time; why?

If you have wondered about these questions or others, *Read This Book!* There are more answers here than most of us have known to ask questions about.

Leni and Jill have had remarkable life changing experiences from which they learned about ancestral healing, receiving messages of light, soul families, spirit guides, and so much more. Within the pages of this book, these women open many windows and provide wonderful insights. These enable us to recognize our own divine light, the light that dwells within each of us. And as we grow in spiritual understanding, we enable those around us to grow as well. And our lives become more beautiful each day.

Thank you Leni and Jill for sharing your love with all of us!

Peny Gallogly, RMP KRMT MITP CCMP ISET

Your work is absolutely correct. Your words gave me chills…meanin⸱
What wonderful synchronicities, as we are all working toward er⸱
of our earth home.

Andre Ferrella, Internationally Acclaimed Visionary Artist
www.Andre.Ferrella.com

These women are authentic, compassionate and passionate about sharing what life has provided them in wisdom, light, healing, love and miracles. Over a year ago I asked the universe to lead me to a tribe of like-minded individuals. I stumbled upon Jilliana and a small group of her colleagues. I had one brief exposure to her and this group of healer/light workers before Covid shut down our worlds.

Fortunately for me it did not stop her drive to continue the desire to spread messages of love and hope. I participated in several on line programs where I also got to meet Leni and hear her perspective on these topics. I always learn something new, while simultaneously validating what I know to be true. At times I don't always understand everything, but in some deep subconscious level it resonates with my intuition.

The meditations I have participated in have impacted my own vibrational energy. I am so excited that they are trying to capture these tidbits in their new joint writing venture. I am grateful to be connected to Leni and Jilliana and offer prayers that this book will touch the lives of many just as they have already blessed mine.

Noel Holdsworth
DNH, PMH ARNP-BC, CARN-AP, CTTS

Additional Titles available on Amazon

The New Covenants:
Spiritual Laws for Transformational Living
Jilliana Raymond

Life is a Spiritual Soup
Discovering Your Spiritual Legacy

AWARD-WINNING
2010 INTERNATIONAL BOOK AWARDS
FINALIST

NOW ON AMAZON

Jilliana Raymond

God's Toolbox:
How God Answers Prayers

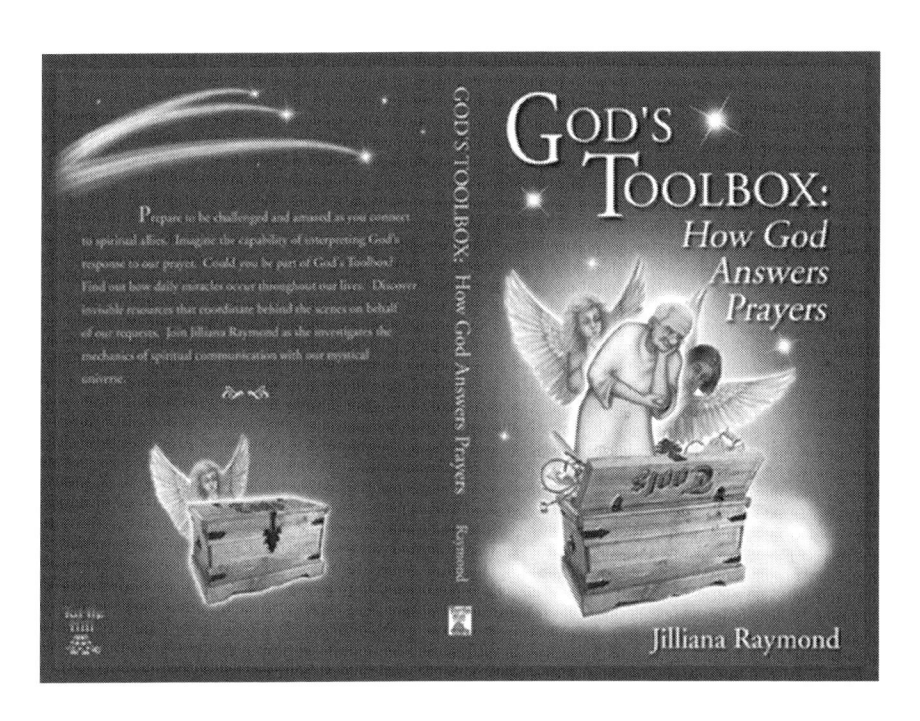

Prepare to be challenged and amused as you connect to spiritual allies. Imagine the capability of interpreting God's response to our prayer. Could you be part of God's Toolbox? Find out how daily miracles occur throughout our lives. Discover invisible resources that coordinate behind the scenes on behalf of our requests. Join Jilliana Raymond as she investigates the mechanics of spiritual communication with our mystical universe.

Jilliana Raymond

Printed in Great Britain
by Amazon